GISELA KONOPKA *received her doctorate in Social Welfare from Columbia University and is Professor of Social Work at the University of Minnesota. The author of* THERAPEUTIC GROUP WORK WITH CHILDREN, GROUP WORK IN THE INSTITUTION, LINDEMAN AND SOCIAL WORK PHILOSOPHY, *and* SOCIAL GROUP WORK: A HELPING PROCESS, *among other books and numerous articles in professional journals, Dr. Konopka has also served as consultant to many child welfare services and guidance clinics both in this country and abroad.*

THE ADOLESCENT GIRL IN CONFLICT

G I S E L A   K O N O P K A

Prentice-Hall, Inc., Englewood Cliffs, New Jersey

To

Those Who Care

This book is based on a three-year research project financed by a grant MH-5-R11-01055 of the National Institute of Mental Health

Current printing (last number):

10

FOREWORD

This short book of large dimensions identifies for the first time the specific problems *peculiar to girls* that lead to the misbehavior of most girls who are officially tagged and handled as delinquents. In other words, by offering the first systematic and usable theory of the causation of delinquency in girls in our society—it helps to substantially increase our understanding of all adolescent girls. This book opens the way for the extension of the emancipation of women to the girls who violate the laws and mores of our society and, as an inevitable by-product, to the great mass of women in the lower income classes. It blasts the hypocrisy and injustice of the double standard. It challenges the capacity of the middle class administration of criminal justice for children and youth—police, judges, probation officers, training-school personnel including social workers and teachers—to work effectively with officially recognized delinquent girls or boys, the great majority of whom come from the lower income classes. It shames us all for our inhumanity. Only a woman could have written this book—only a woman of exceptional experience, warmth, insight, and skill.

In a society which values property rather than people, it is perhaps inevitable that most students of delinquency and crime should focus on boy offenders to the neglect of girls. For offending girls appear to represent a comparatively minor threat to property and to public comfort. Nationwide juvenile court statistics regularly report one girl delinquent to four, five, or six boys. Furthermore, the majority of offenses by boys year after year involves some kind of theft or destruction of property, whereas most girls are charged with delinquency because of sexual misbehavior, whether so identified or listed as truancy, running away, or being ungovernable or incorrigible.

Even on the level of society's property interests there is some evidence that this underevaluation of the girl offender may be shortsighted. A recent study of poverty areas in Minneapolis by that city's Youth Development Project revealed that girl delinquents numbered not one to five boys, but one to two. Moreover, as Dr. Konopka makes clear, their girl companions often play a decisive role in pushing vulnerable boys and gangs into or steering them away from delinquent acts. She also reminds us that delinquent girls are or will become mothers. The community, by its understanding and treatment or its lack thereof, largely determines whether these girls will mother future delinquents or law-abiding and useful citizens.

The suffering and loss that concern Dr. Konopka and "Those Who Care," to whom she dedicates this book, are the human suffering and loss. Surely no writer has communicated this more effectively or more poignantly. Her principal instrument is the girls' own words taken down in private interviews, in group therapy sessions, or expressed in diaries, poems, and letters. This is, of course, the "own story" technique used so extensively with delinquent boys by Clifford Shaw and, in a more fragmentary way, with delinquent girls by W. I. Thomas and others, and pioneered in diagnosis of delinquent children by Healy and Bronner. Emphasizing the value of the "own story" in revealing the emotional attitudes, conflicts, dreams, and inner mental life, Healy and Bronner had this to say:

> No study of delinquents that is either scientific or practical from the standpoint of treatment can be undertaken without getting at the facts which can only be obtained through the individual's own story well guided by sympathetic questioning. It requires more technical understanding and training than perhaps any other part of the study.*

To such training and understanding Dr. Konopka adds the ability to win the complete confidence of these disillusioned and suspicious girls: to listen to them not only with her mind but with her heart and without condemning—in short, to see through their eyes. As a result, the girls' own words, which make up the largest part of this book, not only give significant and often horrifying details of the brutality, rejection, and injustice most have known, but also lay bare the hopeless loneliness and romantic illusions with which they hide their fruitless search for love, their self-contempt, their thwarted ambitions and abilities, and the facelessness of the self-

* Healy, William and Augusta F. Bronner, *New Light on Delinquency and Its Treatment.* New Haven: Yale University Press, 1936.

righteous adult world. Although the author, with the girls' permission, checked their official records, the facts and emotions poured into her sympathetic ear ring too true to need verification.

These "own" stories show up the inadequacies of the typical case history made by juvenile courts, which guides the dispositions of delinquent girls, the supervisory activities of probation officers, and the treatment programs followed by training schools. Perhaps this inadequacy is inevitable in view of the rare skill necessary to the investigator, the limited time available for each case to the writers and users of the case histories, and the general ignorance of the realities of life among the poor which middle class officials bring to their work with delinquent girls and boys. A major service of this book is that it can reduce that inadequacy by opening the eyes of judges, probation officers, and all others concerned to the major factors behind most delinquent behavior by girls.

Since better understanding of the adolescent girl in conflict in our society inevitably dictates more effective methods of care and treatment, the author outlines the major elements of a treatment program. Her recommendations include a new approach to unmarried mothers; the transformation of most training schools so that they will restore instead of further tearing down the girls' self-respect; greater use of social group work, the effectiveness of which she demonstrates. In showing up the inconsistency and futility of parole requirements that forbid parolees to maintain the friendships built up in the institutions, she calls for a reexamination of all services to delinquents.

Just as this study of the adolescent girl in conflict deepens understanding of all adolescent girls, so the resulting treatment and prevention program involves steps that will benefit all children and vast numbers of girls and women who are not in open conflict with society. Because delinquency and crime in any society are functions of its total culture, their prevention and control require major modifications of the culture.

To take but one of several examples, Dr. Konopka's studies of delinquent girls revealed first that the door of opportunity is closed to practically all of them, regardless of their abilities and ambitions; secondly, it showed that these girls have no tradition of preparing by education for careers, but that most of them hope instead for a good marriage to rescue them from the hard and under-paid physical labor as waitresses, servants, scrub women, or factory hands which, for most who are forced to be self-supporting, is the only alternative to prostitution. Dr. Konopka came to see that her delinquent girls suffered these economic frustrations and the related attitudes not because they were delinquent but because nearly all were members of lower-income groups. They belonged to that large segment of the female population which has always been condemned to drudgery and for whom the concept of emancipation of women remains, as yet, quite meaningless. Until our culture opens the door to all jobs and to training, therefore, the denial of equality and status will continue to push many adolescent girls into delinquent behavior.

In the Foreword to *The Unadjusted Girl,* by William I. Thomas published in 1923, Mrs. Ethel S. Dummer wrote of "the farce of our dual system of morality" and praised lines of research "which would lead to less unjust treatment than is at present accorded so-called delinquent women, by changing public opinion and especially altering procedure in our courts, jails and hospitals." It is a disturbing thought that she might have been writing of the situation and the need today, 42 years later, and of Dr. Konopka's studies and purposes. But if it is to survive, our society must, however tardily, find solutions to its major problems and further the humanization of man. Dr. Konopka has forged the sharpest goal and guide to action on behalf of the adolescent girl in conflict and of unemancipated womankind that we have yet seen.

JOHN R. ELLINGSTON
Professor Emeritus
University of Minnesota

ACKNOWLEDGMENTS

This book is written in the hope that it will increase understanding of girls in difficulties and action for better community services. My thanks for help with it should go to very many people. I can single out only a few.

The major thanks go to all the girls who were willing to share with me in an unusually frank way, their concerns, their feelings, and their thoughts. Some of them contributed poetry of real literary value. I am sorry that their names have to be withheld. All of them should know, however, how deeply I appreciate their help and how my respect for them increased as I worked with them.

Another large part of my appreciation goes to organizations: the National Institute of Mental Health financed this three-year study and encouraged me by showing confidence in what I was trying to do. The University of Minnesota granted me one year free from teaching duties to enable me to collect materials. The Department of Corrections, State of Minnesota, permitted me to interview girls confined to its state institutions and facilitated the collection of material in many other ways; its administrators showed a deep concern for this work. Three Minnesota organizations—the St. Paul Diocesan Bureau of Catholic Charities, the Lutheran Social Service of Minnesota and the Salvation Army, St. Paul—which sponsor homes for unmarried mothers permitted me to interview in the homes located in the Twin Cities area as well as to discuss my thoughts and problems with their staffs. Big Sisters' Association, Minneapolis, let me work with a group of its clients.

Thanks go also to many social group workers and caseworkers from different agencies in the Twin Cities who were willing to share their own experiences with me and to think through what I thought I found.

A good friend, Walter Friedlander of the University of California, helped with special interest and a view toward the international scene.

I was fortunate in having the assistance of three excellent readers who helped much with the polishing of the manuscript: Professor Dorothy Sheldon, University of Minnesota; Brother Aquinas Thomas, F.S.C., Manhattan College, New York City, and Mrs. Willis Salisbury, an active participant in community activities in Minneapolis.

My most important deepest thanks must go to two people who have given untold hours of thinking and support: Mrs. Vernie-Mae L. Czaky, my extraordinarily capable research associate, who has helped not only in the collecting of the materials and the reading of the manuscript, but whose constant challenge of the ideas expressed have made this inquiry a much more valuable one than it could have been without her unstinting effort.

The other person to whom special thanks must go is my husband, Paul Konopka. He was able to accept the agitated and sometimes depressed nights that followed my contacts with the girls, the frequently upset evenings when some of them telephoned and asked for additional help, and the labor of many evenings and long weekends of writing and rewriting.

And, of course, no work can be accomplished without the routine and sometimes tedious work that goes into transcribing the recordings of interviews and group sessions and the typing and retyping of the manuscript. My thanks here go to Joan Greguson, Sue Newhall, Diane Hyatt, and Patricia Noer.

GISELA KONOPKA

CONTENTS

Contents

1. THE STUDY

How shall I write? As simply as I can because the deepest truth is the most simply stated. I must write from the heart—cor ad cor loquitur.[1]

The cool mountain air, the blue sky, the sun, the rocks, the olive trees are around us while we sit high above Athens. My Greek lawyer–social-worker friend, taking her eyes off the calm beauty around us, turns to me, "Tell me about your study of the girl in conflict. Do you know that our social workers sometimes still have to rescue a girl from actual threat of death just because she has become illegitimately pregnant? The problem here is just as prevalent as in your country, but much of it is hidden."

And these words came from an earnest young man in Israel, "Certainly we too have street-corner gangs here. The older generation always speaks about the grand old times they had when they built this country. They blame youth now for not being idealistic enough and not showing the pioneer spirit. Our young people resent it and ask, 'What have you left for us to do?' The boys hang around and are angry, but some of them we can help. We know less about what to do with the girls who are in trouble."

My telephone rings often now. Sometimes twice a day, the voice at the other end says, "How are you? I just had to call *somebody!*" And then it continues, "I'm getting along all right. I've found work." Or, "The baby cries; she drives me crazy. What can I do?" Or, "My husband left me and I can't get any of my clothes. Is there anyone who can help?" And again, "I just need someone to talk to." It is always the same girl. Released from a delinquency institution,

[1] Morris L. West, *The Shoes of the Fisherman* (New York: William Morrow & Co., 1963), p. 105. Copyright © 1963 by Morris L. West and reprinted by permission of the author.

after having been in and out of them for years, she is trying to make a home for herself and her child. She struggles. She feels helpless. The worst thing to face is loneliness—and so she calls.

As long as the world has existed, every generation has had difficulties understanding the next one. As long as the world has existed, the young have accused the old of not understanding, and the old have accused the young of being frivolous and inconsiderate. But our time cannot—and does not—want to be satisfied with knowing that this has always been the case. Just as man has learned to tame natural forces by understanding how they work, man now also wants to better understand himself and other people. Why? There are many reasons: the basic thirst for knowledge, the hope to gain power over others, and the genuine wish to help. "Am I my brother's keeper?" The imperative implied in this question is not an invention of the twentieth century.

But the twentieth century demands better knowledge of how to help, not only for the sake of the individual in trouble but also for the sake of the whole society. When societies were feudalistic or lived under benevolent or harsh dictatorships, the individual did not matter much. Decisions were made only by those in power. To them the "people" were predominantly "hands," and the only concern was that there should be enough of them to do the necessary work and fight the battles. In modern democratic societies, society as a whole is dependent on citizens who vote, on people who can think through important issues, on mothers who can raise children intelligently and lovingly, on young people who will act out of a feeling of responsibility and thought. This makes the relationships between generations a vital issue for the survival of this kind of a society.

Several years ago, after Cohen published his book on boy gangs,[2] after Salisbury so vividly described the violence in New York City streets,[3] after Hathaway and Monachesi made their excellent studies on delinquency,[4] and after Cloward and Ohlin[5] published their

[2] Albert K. Cohen, *Delinquent Boys* (New York: Free Press of Glencoe, Inc., 1955).

[3] Harrison E. Salisbury, *The Shook-up Generation* (New York: Harper & Row, Publishers, Inc., 1958).

[4] Starke R. Hathaway and Elio D. Monachesi, "The Personalities of Predelinquent Boys," *Journal of Criminal Law, Criminology and Police Science,* 48: 2 (July-August 1957), 149-63.

Starke R. Hathaway and Elio D. Monachesi, *Adolescent Personality and Behavior—MMPI Patterns of Normal, Delinquent, Dropout, and Other Outcomes* (Minneapolis: University of Minnesota Press, 1963).

Starke R. Hathaway, Elio D. Monachesi, and Lawrence A. Young, "Delin-

thesis on lack of opportunity as a factor in delinquency, I began to raise the question: "What about the *girl* in trouble? What do we know about her? How can we help her?" I talked with several of these authors. Each one said "We *should* know about them. We haven't studied much about them because the number of delinquent girls seems to be so much smaller than the number of delinquent boys, but we should know." We all agreed that girls seem to be much more influential—both negatively and positively—in relation to delinquent behavior than appears on the surface. Some individual or gang fights among boys start because of rivalry over girls. One girl told me:

> They fought about me. I just sat on the stairs one day. Eric passed by. He said, "I'll pull you down the stairs." I told my boy-friend John about that. Then they fought. They always fight over girls.

The War of Troy, the duels of the knights of the Middle Ages, are repeated in the many dark streets of our cities.

Another girl, giving the other side of the picture, said to me, "When we are around, the boys don't get drunk. Then they don't steal cars." This was borne out by fact in her peer group.

Finally, the girl is especially important for the influence she will have on the next generation as the future mother of children.

Really significant and helpful work with girls in trouble is hampered by lack of knowledge. In my own years of work in child guidance clinics, general youth work, neighborhood centers, treatment centers, and correctional institutions, I found that there seemed to be a general feeling of bewilderment among the personnel about the girls they worked with. Often there was an unusually rigid handling of these girls, a generally unimaginative program for them in institutions. The attitude of the public and of the personnel who worked with delinquent girls was predominantly one of deep resentment. Practices in institutions for delinquent boys were also often cruel and punishing, yet one found frequently an attitude of patience and toleration: "We can work with them. Boys will be boys." I almost never found this philosophy when it came to delinquent girls.

I have also been struck by the *complexity* of the problem of the

---

quency Rates and Personality," *Journal of Criminal Law, Criminology and Police Science,* 40: 5 (January-February 1960), 433-40.
[5] Richard A. Cloward and Lloyd E. Ohlin, *Delinquency and Opportunity* (New York: Free Press of Glencoe, Inc., 1960).

adolescent girl who in one way or another shows behavior unacceptable in our society. Almost invariably her problems are
deeply personalized. Whatever her offense—whether shoplifting,
truancy, or running away from home—it is usually accompanied
by some disturbance or unfavorable behavior in the sexual area,
thus involving her own total being and affecting her relationships
with others. This totality of involvement has an influence on her
own confusion and makes many people shy away from her problems.

The sexual behavior of the delinquent girl hits close to the personal feelings of most people, especially women. They know about
—though they sometimes deny—their own longings, their own
struggles, their own fears. Sometimes they may also be tempted to
steal from a counter at a department store, but this impulse is less
personal, less universal than the sex impulse. Thus, the defenses
against the sex impulse are stronger, and the denial greater. It is no
accident that negative stereotypes of minority groups are always
closely related to sex behavior. In fact, those who want to foster
hatred of such groups use sex behavior as a deliberate weapon. The
most ugly accusation made against Jews under the Nazi regime—
and the most inflammatory one—concerned the imputed lust of the
Jewish male and his wish to sexually assault the innocent, blonde
Germanic maiden. Hitler's "race laws" were based on this charge;
so was the pornographic publication, *Der Stürmer,* used so effectively against the Jews. We know that this same hidden fear of sex
is still used in the hate propaganda directed against minority racial
groups, especially Negroes. Some of this "unnamed horror" is present in much of the talk about delinquency in girls and in trans-
lated into the almost unbelievably neglectful—and sometimes cruel
—treatment of these girls in many institutions and communities.

My motivation to study the girl in conflict, then, came from
wanting to understand, wanting to help, wanting to change institutional practice and community attitudes.

One of this century's great insights into the human being came
through Sigmund Freud's clinical work and the theories he drew
from it.[6] In his long life he himself was willing to look critically at
his theory and to change it when he found it necessary. Some of
his great students—either in sharp conflict with the master or building creatively on his work—have added to or changed his theory.
Erik H. Erikson especially has contributed considerably by com-

[6] Sigmund Freud, *A General Introduction to Psychoanalysis* (New York: Boni
& Liveright, 1924).

bining knowledge from cultural anthropology with Freud's topography of the individual.[7] He stresses that one must understand the human being not only as an inseparable whole of body, soul, and intellect, but also as part of a process of interaction with others and with his total environment.

When I began this study of the adolescent girl in conflict, my aim was twofold:

A. To make a contribution to the *understanding* of the adolescent girl in conflict as a total person in her own particular cultural environment through a study of her values, her goals, her attitudes toward adults, her emotional relationships with peers, her voluntary group associations, her impact on related group structures (i.e., boy gangs), her outlets for her inner drives, and her image of herself.

B. To demonstrate helpful treatment of girls, with special emphasis on the use of the *social group work method*, on the basis of my assumption that mental health is most heavily influenced by interaction among human beings, and that the peer group is most vital to the formation of attitudes and self-image in the adolescent.[8]

I expected that the results of my study would:

1. Add to general knowledge of adolescents, especially the adolescent girl.

2. Help improve methods for the care and treatment of disturbed and delinquent girls, individually and in groups.

3. Contribute to new and constructive programs in institutions for delinquent and disturbed girls.

4. Contribute tangible suggestions to community programs working with adolescent girls.

I would have liked to have studied a cross section of all adolescent girls—and I still hope to do so some day. But this would take years, and I felt I had to start with those who are of greatest concern to the community. I therefore chose to look at those girls in conflict who had been adjudicated delinquent or who had become unwed mothers and sought refuge in homes for unmarried mothers. I was sure that in trying to understand them and to work with them we would gain much knowledge of girls in general, since there is no sharp line between those who act out their conflicts

---

[7] Erik H. Erikson, *Childhood and Society* (New York: W. W. Norton and Company, Inc., 1950).

[8] Gisela Konopka, "A Healthy Group Life—Social Group Work's Contribution to Mental Health," *Mental Hygiene,* 45: 3 (July 1961), 327-35.

directly and in forms unacceptable to society and all others who struggle with them at some time in their lives, but do not act in this particular way.

It is *We* one studies when one studies any part of the human race, never *They*.

Theories Regarding Delinquent Behavior Related to the Study

> *Ich sah, wenn ich ihn recht verstand, Er ist ein Narr auf eigne Hand.* (I saw, if I understood him right, that he is a fool of his own making.)

The above quotation from Goethe refers to a pompous little man who boasted of being totally original in his thinking and findings. But too much research regarding human beings and too much research into human relations or descriptions of various forms of therapeutic intervention are done as if nothing similar had preceded them. Often such work is proclaimed as completely new only because the investigators did not first take the time to learn what others had done and then build upon that. They think it is important to be totally original.

Although I thought at first that little had been written about the girl in conflict, an intensive study of the literature showed that some material was available, and the appended bibliography will allow the reader a glimpse of it. There are reams of material on delinquency. Before starting my investigation, I had to look at some of the theories advanced to explain delinquent behavior, even though they were concerned mostly with boys. Let me share some of these theories and some of my thinking about them, so that my own evolving theory—and perhaps my bias—will be known.

Talcott Parsons, in his *Essays in Sociological Theory*, says that the Western family is female centered, that delinquency in the boy is a protest against this and the outcome of his difficulty in finding someone with whom he can identify.[9] But in saying that the girl has

[9] Talcott Parsons, *Essays in Sociological Theory, Pure and Applied*, second ed. (New York: Free Press of Glencoe, Inc., 1954). For a refutation of Parsons' argument see Cloward and Ohlin, *op. cit.*

a more favorable opportunity for emotional maturing, because she has her mother before her eyes and can identify with the functions of a housewife and mother, Parsons completely disregards the occurrence of delinquency or conflict in girls. It seems obvious that he oversimplifies the girl's position, omits the generally changing status of women, and, especially, does not take into account the personality of the mother, the significance of the absence of the father, and the development of the girl. Furthermore, his study is mostly restricted to a middle-class model of family relationships.

The Bloch and Niederhoffer theory places much of the responsibility for adolescent misbehavior on the long postponement of adult roles.[10] I personally think that this theory does not stand up in a period of prosperity and early marriages and again relates only to an advantaged part of the population, but even if it were acceptable, it was presented by Bloch and Niederhoffer exclusively in relation to the boy and his frustration at not being able to take on the roles of husband and breadwinner. It may apply as a parallel to the college girl who also experiences this postponement, probably intensified by her own confusion as to whether she should prepare to be a wife and mother or a breadwinner or both. But the girl in lower economic groups faces very different problems.

Cloward and Ohlin have advanced one of the most recent theories, which is based on Robert K. Merton's hypothesis that deviant behavior occurs when there is a serious discrepancy between the aspiration toward goals which are considered necessary to success in a given society and the opportunities for achieving them.[11] I consider this theory very fruitful, but the dimension of personality factors cannot be omitted in trying to understand delinquency. Also: What are the goals that our society presents to young people, particularly to girls? Cloward and Ohlin cite an example of cultural differences in goal aspiration between children of Jewish and Italian immigrants. They refer to a study by Toby which presents the fact that Jewish youth place a high value on learning.[12] Why? Because their culture had for centuries given prestige to the scholar. Second-generation Jewish children therefore studied diligently. As Toby puts it, "Two thousand years of preparation lay behind them." The Italian youth, on the contrary, have no such tradition of study to

[10] Herbert A. Bloch and Arthur Niederhoffer, *The Gang: A Study in Adolescent Behavior* (New York: Philosophical Library, 1958).

[11] Cloward and Ohlin, *op. cit.*

[12] Jackson Toby, "Hoodlum or Businessman: An American Dilemma" in Marshall Sklare, ed., *The Jews: Social Patterns of an American Group* (New York: Free Press of Glencoe, Inc., 1958).

fall back on. This influence of tradition on the content of aspirations is very significant. A question of such influence arises in relation to female youth. How old is the tradition of study, of preparation for a vocation, profession, or employment in general for girls? There always have been working women, but systematic job preparation is recent. Can this partially explain the lack of concern for school in many girls, or the frequent absence of goal direction related to future employment? Is the "thwarted ambition" or "lack of opportunity" theory as valid for girls as for boys as a basic explanation of delinquency?

None of these three theories seems totally satisfactory for understanding and working productively with the girl in conflict. They grew out of work with boys and observation of boys. Will we find another theory, more precise, more helpful to practice? This was the focus of my search.

I tried to start out with as open a mind as possible. I hesitated to advance a hypothesis for my study because so little focus had been given to girls. I had a hunch that better understanding would accrue out of a better view of the culture conflict in which the girl finds herself—but I did not want to pre-influence my study by singling out this factor for research. I am convinced that much research into understanding of human beings has been hampered rather than advanced by a limited approach dictated by a preconceived theory. Will you, reader, follow me along this rather uncharted voyage until we begin to discern the markers, perceive a "Gestalt" (entity)?

Method of Study

> *As I progressed, I found that the closer and deeper I looked, the more I saw and the more there was to see. When I couldn't see any more, the deficiency was mine.*[13]

"The only boast man can claim: that nothing more complicated than he is to be found among molecular groupings," [14] wrote the biologist, Jean Rostand.

The adventure into a deepened understanding of human beings is one of the most exciting projects one can undertake, and because of man's complexity and the subjectivity of the media we must use, one of the most difficult. Even though the tools by which we explore the physical world are not wholly objective—Einstein has shaken the belief in absolute objectivity in this realm—they are more so than the means available for understanding human beings, which are always related to human judgment, even when so-called objective tests are used. One has to be aware of this limitation when one tries to understand others. How can one ever really enter into the emotions, feelings, or thoughts of another person? And how can one ever generalize about the infinite variety of humanity? One of the girls interviewed said, "There's no use trying to explain ourselves to anybody even if they say they want to help us. They know everything beforehand. They have read the books." Therefore, the first rule of my approach to my investigation was a firm *don't* to myself: Don't start with any preconceived notion of what the girl in conflict is, thinks, feels, or wants to achieve. You cannot help being influenced by some of your own experiences or the theories which have become part of your work. Make them explicit to yourself so that you can look at them critically. And, above all, *listen.* Do not discard whatever the girls may say as something that does not fit into some theory. Do not say or think too quickly, "She is

---

[13] Wayne Miller, *The World Is Young* (New York: Ridge Press, Inc., 1958), p. 7. Reprinted by permission.

[14] Jean Rostand, *The Substance of Man* (New York: Doubleday and Company, Inc., 1962).

just covering up" or "She is projecting" or "She means just the op-posite of what she says." (These were attitudes I found frequently in the so-called "diagnosis" entered into the records of the delin-quents I interviewed.) Listen carefully and then try to draw con-clusions.

Wayne Miller, who explored childhood through photography, wrote in the introduction to one of his books:

> A perceptive man once said that "to look at the world through the eyes of another would be true knowledge." This is what I have attempted here. For three years I have tried to look with children rather than at them, and to see through their eyes—and in their forms and faces—the sense and meaning of the experiences that crowd each day when the world is young.[15]

Wayne Miller's words also characterize my attempt to understand the adolescent girl in conflict. If true knowledge can only be found by looking at the world through the eyes of the girls themselves, how could I find it unless I too saw with their eyes? I could not use a checklist or a questionnaire. If I wanted to really understand and comprehend the feelings of the girls, their value systems, their true goals (not the ones they think they should present to the adult world that has power over them), then I had to gain their con-fidence. I knew that I could attain this only by a form of living with them, by a modification of the field method of the anthropolo-gist. I therefore stayed in some of the institutions for two or three days at a time over a period of three months.[16] I ate with the girls, helped them wash dishes, and was in their cottages at certain hours when they were off duty. I was not "one of the girls" to them, but I was an unusual adult in their particular environment. I had no power over them; I had no favors to hand out. I was no "mystery" either. They were completely and honestly informed about why I was with them. Prior to my coming I had, with the permission of the institutional authorities, sent a letter to each girl, telling her about my interest in knowing more about adolescent girls who had got into difficulties, about my intent to learn as much as possible. Here is a sample of such a letter:

---

[15] Wayne Miller, *op. cit.*, p. 4.

[16] The institutions used were a delinquency training school and a women's reformatory in which I saw only the adolescent girls.

September 4, 1962

Dear Friend:

Perhaps you have met me before, when I visited The School. I am teaching at the University of Minnesota. I have worked a lot with young people who have had some difficulties in their lives. I have found increasingly that we know very little about girls. We adults talk much about them, but we seldom have an opportunity to hear really what the girl herself thinks.

All girls have their dreams and wishes, their likes and dislikes. They usually talk about all this among themselves. I have been very fortunate to have the opportunity to take one year away from my job and spend some time at The School just to listen to you. I hope you can consider me as your friend. Nothing you say will go into your records. I come only to listen and to learn. I will be at The School every Monday and Tuesday from September to the end of December.

I may not be able to listen to all of you, but I look forward to talking to some of you. I will appreciate your help. Thank you and best wishes.

Sincerely,
(Mrs.) Gisela Konopka, D.S.W.

The girls knew that I had talked to the personnel of the institution and that the staff was informed about the reasons for my being there. My position, as a "special" person, as an outsider without power, but a participant in their lives, helped me become a confidante.

I went with the girls through such odd rigid ceremonies of their institutional life as waiting silently in line for the door to the dining room to open. I sat with them in a locked room because the housemother had to leave the cottage. I was present when they waited eagerly for mail and I saw those who expected a letter turn away in mute despair when they received nothing.

I sat at a table with four coldly hostile girls, three of them pregnant, who wolfed down rich food, though they knew they should diet. I heard their suppressed, "Who cares anyhow? We can't keep the baby." I sat at the bed of one of those three, crying her heart out because she was afraid: "Who will be with me when I have the baby?"

I sat in a locked cell on a bare cot next to a girl deprived of her regular clothing day and night because she had tried to escape. I watched her show off her pretended indifference while her eyes glittered with unshed tears. And I saw her change into an anxious and frightened child when the dusk came and I had to leave. She asked with a small voice if I would lend her a comb to fix her unkempt hair and if I would pull the blanket over her. I heard her admit for the first time—what to her was weakness—"I am alone, I am so afraid."

I sat on the steps in a cottage and shared the girls' enthusiasm about the art teacher who had let them make a model of their dreamhouses. What gifted architects some of them proved to be! And how much yearning for beauty and comfort was poured into those models!

I watched a pretty fourteen-year-old dance in, with stars in her eyes, wearing a new coat she had just received from the institution because she was to be released the next day, and I saw others surrounding her with that mixture of envy and generous admiration so typical of any teenage girl.

This "living with" the girls was the essential background for more formal individual interviews and for a series of group sessions with a small number of specifically selected youngsters. To make the girls as comfortable as possible the interviews were usually held in the living quarters. I began by referring to my letter, then explained again the absolute confidentiality of anything that was brought out. I told the girls that I would write about them but never about one personally or using her name. I asked permission, which was given in most cases, to take notes or to turn on my tape recorder. Sometimes the tape recorder inhibited a girl too much, and I turned it off. When I made notes, I dictated from them immediately or on the next day, so that the narrative would record as accurately as possible what the girl had said. I told the girls that they could start to talk about whatever was on their minds, but most of the time they wanted a specific question. I usually started the interviews with an individual girl by saying, "If you had an opportunity to stand on the rooftop or a street corner and shout at the world about what you think it does not seem to understand about you or your young friends, and about what makes you unhappy, what would you shout? Just shoot!"

Only rarely did a girl not respond to this open-ended request. Most of the time the flow of narrative took an hour or more. If the spontaneous account did not contain answers to some of the specific areas I wanted to have covered, I threw in questions such as the following:

> Was there ever in your life an adult whom you really trusted?
> Do you, or did you, have friends? What kinds?
> Have you ever belonged to any kind of an organized group?
> What are things you like to do?

What would you like to do if you were not here?

What would you like your life to be like when you grow up, let's say when you are twenty or twenty-four years old? (In the beginning I said "thirty years," but soon learned that this is practically old age to a teenager, and too far to look ahead.)

I asked the girls for diaries or poetry, and those who wanted to shared them with me. The interviews were supplemented by an examination of the case histories of the girls concerned, with their own permission and that of the agency which served them. Very few refused permission. Those who did are not included in this study.

It was touching and almost miraculous to see how open the girls were, how very seldom they purposely distorted their stories, how hungry they were to talk to someone who would listen without penalizing them for their confidence. I could not help but think of a practice in the Middle Ages: Then the Church building was reserved as a neutral place of refuge for one who was persecuted by the law. There he could rest his exhausted body and soul and be free for a short time. The person of the researcher represented something like this. Though the intent of the interviews was not a helping or therapeutic one, the interviews often had this effect. In the lives of many of these girls an adult who listens is almost unknown.

The group sessions differed from the interviews; they were not conducted for information alone. The girls were frankly informed that the researcher in those sessions was also the social group worker, who would try to help them work through and on their problems, that she would be more active and, if occasion warranted, would enlist resources to help them. All group sessions were recorded and transcribed with the permission of the girls. The sessions were usually so intensive and emotion-laden that the tape recorder was soon forgotten. In the delinquency institution they were held in a comfortable room with a fireplace. The walk through the dark campus from the cottages to the house where the sessions were held, the evening hour, the preparation in the kitchen of warm cocoa and cookies by the girls themselves, the return to the cottages on "one's own honor" in the dark winter night added to the therapeutic influence as much as the actual discussions.

The group of older adolescents in the reformatory met in a more formal setting, around a table in a conference room, but also with coffee and cookies to relax the always tense atmosphere of a closed institution. These girls especially needed to talk, and used every minute of the ten one-and-one-half-hour group sessions.

Two groups were conducted outside the institutional setting. One, a continuation of the group in the delinquency institution, was formed when the girls were released on parole; the other was a group of thirteen- and fourteen-year-olds who were on probation and had never been in an institution. The latter was the only group which did not meet under the auspices of the court; they were served by a private agency, the Big Sister Association.

Population of the Study

I got to know and listened to 181 adolescent girls between fourteen and nineteen years of age. All of them had acted out their conflicts sufficiently to come to the attention of the courts or private social agencies. The majority of them (100) had been adjudicated delinquent, and were either in an institution for delinquents, in a reformatory, on probation, or on parole.

A smaller number of girls (76) was also in institutions, but only because they were unwed pregnant girls who, for various reasons, could not or would not have their babies in their own community. They were a more middle-class group to whom—and in whose environment—illegitimate pregnancy was so unacceptable that they had to use the institution as a hiding place. Most of the girls I saw were Caucasian—as typical for Minnesota—but among them were also Indian and Negro youngsters.

The United States, with its variety of landscapes, immigrant groups, and state development, does not have one "typical" population. No geographically limited study can represent the total country. Minnesota, the state in which I did my study, has large, highly industrialized cities with a population of various nationality and racial backgrounds. It has small towns, some of which are beginning to bulge and others suffering decline. There is a relatively homogeneous population, but there are also pockets of minority groups. The state has not the extremes of the overwhelming population problems of Chicago or New York or Detroit. But it has its share of them. Findings coming from such a state are characteristic for a large part of this continent.

I have talked about a "study" and "findings" and I have rows of heavy volumes of collected material and a whole library of tapes. Yet the content is not paper and ink or electrical impressions on a glossy band. The content is:

Dora, with her skin breaking out because "I am so nervous," and her defiant song:

> I no longer use my mind,
> Nor think of anything.
> For I am just a puppet,
> and my master pulls the strings.
>
> There's just one thing about it
> I fear he doesn't know:
> Strings are easily broken
> and then he'll have to go.

It is Judy, with her large brown eyes, her hair messed up and tinted, who wants to be "somebody, just somebody who proves to people that a girl can be somebody, even if she was here in the institution."

It is Bertha, broad, peasant-like, and with violent temper, who fought like a lioness to keep her out-of-wedlock child:

> When I had my little baby, it was one of the happiest moments of my life. I want to keep her more than anything else in this world. She is the only thing I am able to cling to; my only hope of ever changing or doing something worthwhile in my life.

It is Joanne, fingernails bitten, always in trouble, always stealing, and yet a child:

> I know I'm here to be punished, but still, I feel I should be able to have a few things for the enjoyment and pleasure of doing them. I like to be outside. I know a lot of the other girls do. A lot of times we are cooped up inside. This isn't easy either. We can't explode right out in the open to the girls when we get mad. It isn't easy when things have to build inside of you, and you can't let them out.

It is Donna, who does not dare share her dreams of becoming a doctor, because "Indians don't get anywhere."

It is Stella, who cusses and hates and glares so that you cringe, because you don't know how to explain or how to help.

It is Thelma who cries because she is so depressed—and does not know why—three days after giving birth to a child who is no longer with her.

It is Leda, who hates all white people; who says as she shyly puts her head on your shoulder—a white woman's shoulder—when the evening falls, "Help me. Stay, I am afraid."

The "study" is people.

In the sleepless nights which usually accompanied my contacts with the girls, the cry of one of them rang in my ears, "If only someone would listen!" Listening does not always mean agreeing, but listening—and listening with compassion—is necessary to comprehend human beings.

By talking openly and listening honestly the girls themselves, together with those who are willing to hear, may help push the frontiers of understanding of all human beings a small step ahead. Perhaps this study will help to move our communities a little closer to better treatment of girls in trouble. Perhaps this will enable them to find ways of preventing some of the more serious conflicts. The girls need to be heard, not only for their own sakes, but for the sake of the total community which can only be a healthy body if it helps *all* its citizens, *all* its youth.

2. THEY
ARE PEOPLE

*Oftentimes have I heard you
speak of one who commits a
wrong as though he were not
one of you, but a stranger unto
you and an intruder upon your
world.*[1]

"I am no more a girl—I am a delinquent." This sentence
was spoken often, with a great variety of feeling. One voice was
bitter. The next was resigned; still another boasting, while some
were defeated or depressed. It always implied that the girl felt that
she had become—or that others thought of her as—a different
species from any other adolescent girl. It was said most frequently
with the hope that it would be contradicted, but sometimes the girl
accepted it and saw herself as "separate," as "outside," with the
stamp of delinquency inexorably impressed upon her. The ones
who felt this way had incorporated into themselves a rather common attitude toward delinquents, and especially toward delinquent
girls. Many people cannot describe what they understand by the
term "delinquency," but they have a vague, unformulated stereotyped picture of the delinquent girl, accompanied by feelings of
disgust, hostility, and distance. It is expressed in the astonished
exclamation by many who have visited a delinquency institution.
"Why, they look just like anyone else!" Or "She can't be delinquent,
she looks so nice." Or "But this is an intelligent girl, she can't be
delinquent."

Pressure to separate the delinquent into a different class from
the rest of the population is influenced partially by an emotional

[1] Kahlil Gibran, *The Prophet* (New York: Alfred A. Knopf, Inc., 1951), p. 40.
Reprinted by permission of the publisher.

need in many people to keep their own integrity intact by denying that they have anything in common with those who seem to be or who are "bad." It is also based on the genuine wish to categorize, to find the specific characteristic of what produces and indicates delinquency so as to be able to treat or prevent it. This is a legitimate intent of any inquiry into human behavior, its underlying reasons, and the factors that contribute to it. Before Leeuwenhoek's discovery of microbes one knew about illness but not of the existence of bacteria.[2] Only then was some relationship made between illness and those newly discovered phenomena. It took many more years to make the connections between certain kinds of microbes and certain kinds of illnesses. It took even more years to realize that the entrance of a certain microbe into the body does not of itself always produce a certain illness, but that the bodies of different people react differently to the same onslaught, that the violence of the illness—or even its occurrence—is also related to many more factors than the presence of the microbe. Some people exposed to the tuberculosis bacillus develop tuberculosis; some do not. This difference depends on the state of their nourishment, the biological predisposition with which they were born, the housing environment in which they live. We have learned that a whole constellation of factors is needed to produce a certain result in the human body, and yet even in this relatively limited area of the total human being we do not know all the contributing factors. This applies even more to human "states" or behaviors which are not related exclusively to physical functioning. Even if delinquency were a clearly defined entity, a single form of behavior, it would be difficult enough to determine the various contributing factors. But it is not such an entity. It means different behavior—even different acts committed.

Those acts performed by juveniles which are considered delinquent fall into three basic categories:

    a. Those which are considered delinquent regardless of whether committed by a juvenile or an adult, because they violate criminal laws. Examples are stealing or assault on human life.

    b. Those which violate societal morals as agreed upon generally in our particular society, regardless of whether the person is a juvenile or an adult. An example is certain forms of sex behavior.

    c. Those which are violations only because the person is a minor.

[2] Paul DeKruif, *Microbe Hunters* (New York: Harcourt, Brace & World, Inc., 1932), pp. 1-22.

This is exemplified in truancy from school or teenage drinking. These violations are governed by different laws in different states, and therefore will make a youngster a delinquent in one state and not in another.

Delinquent acts of girls fall into all three categories, though most delinquent girls have some problems in relation to sex. This assortment of offenses alone shows that it is impossible to talk about one kind of delinquent personality. Beyond this, the *reasons* for the behavior are even more diversified and highly complex than are the types of behavior. One can only say that those designated as "delinquent" are so by virtue of having been adjudicated as such, which means having been judged by the Court. They are personalities of a wide variety. They have in common that they have come into conflict with the society around them—for many reasons. They are *adolescent* girls and they are individual personalities. They are part of the human race with its common traits and problems. They belong to a subgroup determined by age and sex—adolescent girls —and they belong to this group in our time with its particular impact, because of rapid change and especially the change in the position of women.

As members—not outsiders—of this group, what are their specific characteristics? What contributes to drive them into serious conflict with society? This is our inquiry. Conversely, we must bear in mind they are not only members of a group. Each one of them is unique. In practice, in teaching, in treatment, in child rearing, it is essential that this uniqueness be remembered: that the marvel of the infinite variation among human beings never be forgotten. There are qualities which all human beings have in common, and which make them human, and there are qualities which subgroups have in common, but no one person is exactly the same as another. Kluckhohn and Murray summarized this most clearly when they wrote: "Every man is in certain respects: a) like all other men; b) like some other men; c) like no other man." [3] Whatever may be generalized about delinquent girls, each individual must always be seen and heard, separately and clearly. Whatever may emerge as the general understanding which helps us work better with all adolescent girls, it must be qualified by the awareness that each girl is different and that her plea not to be "treated by the book" must be heeded.

Therefore, before I begin to generalize, I want to let you, the

[3] Clyde Kluckhohn and Henry A. Murray, *Personality in Nature, Society and Culture* (New York: Alfred A. Knopf, Inc., 1949), p. 35.

reader, meet some of the girls through their own words. Some of the following are transcripts from taped accounts, others from notes taken during the interviews. Only names and places are changed to protect the speakers.

If you meet Bertha in the institution on a working day she looks like a sturdy Scandinavian peasant woman, the salt of the earth. She is slightly stocky, with light brown hair and lively blue eyes. When you see her dressed up she is very much a sophisticated city girl with good taste in clothes, but an underlying quality of earthiness still comes through. Bertha's voice is loud but not unpleasant. She is very outspoken toward anyone and her moods of affection or anger are quite violent. Bertha had been attending the group work sessions for several weeks when she gave the following account:

My name is Bertha. My age is nineteen. Right now I'm in the reformatory. I would like to tell you part of my life, and the feelings I have about the things I've done, and the feelings that I have for other people who have tried to help me and who have succeeded and some who have failed. I would like to start at my very early age. I was very unhappy at home and at school and . . . I tried very hard to get along at school or at home, but I didn't care what happened to me at this age. Then when I was around five when I was in school, I had stolen the teacher's check. I know it seems quite silly, but that's what I did. I went to the drugstore, and I had met my brother there, and I told him that I wanted to cash this, and he thought I was very foolish. He told me I would get into a lot of trouble. I told him I didn't care. Well, anyway I had signed my own name instead of the teacher's name. They had called the cops, and the cops had taken me home; me and my brother. And my mother, she, oh, she was mad at me. So, it was almost the end of school that time, and my mother had gone to court for me that June— in June I was to be taken away from her. And she came home from court, and she told me about this. She thought I would be very unhappy about going. No, I wasn't. I was going to be with kids my own age.

So the day had come that I would go and my mother had taken me there. But I can remember before she left I cried like I don't know what. I just didn't want her to leave me. Anyway I got along very well at the Children's Center for the first couple of weeks and when I got to know everybody, I started running around. I loved this Children's Center very much, and I loved the people that had authority there. I had gotten my way a lot of times, and yet in a way I was still unhappy. And I started to run away from there. Even though I had a lot of privileges, I still wasn't satisfied. So then I ran away, and they would bring me back. Sure, I was fine for awhile, and then I would run away again.

So, I had to go to another Children's Center. This one I did not like at all. I was very unhappy there, and I ran away, and I was stealing and smoking and everything.

Finally, I had to go to court for running away and stealing, and I was sentenced to the delinquent institution. When I went there, I was at the age of ten. I didn't care what I did. I started getting into trouble; going with girls. I was there over a year.

They sent me back to the Children's Center. I felt that was a mistake. I had learned too much at the institution. Anyway I didn't get along at the Children's Center, and I was put into a foster home. I loved this foster mother very dearly. But she drank too much, and she and her third husband argued a lot. It didn't work out. I had stayed out late with a girl I had met, and I started getting involved with men.

So I went back to the institution and they revoked my parole. Well, I was quite mad about this, and I told the Board just what they could do with my parole. But then, after I said it and I was punished for it, I felt like a fool; I knew these people cared for me, or they wouldn't take as much time to try and help me as they were doing. Now in the institution I got interested in cosmetology and interpretative dancing and things like that. I did pretty well but still I was getting into trouble.

So then I went out on parole. I started "mixing." [Institutional jargon for dating Negroes.] I was going on fourteen years. I started hustling for a man. Well, when I came to my senses I figured to myself that no man would really want a girl if she would do that, so I left him. I met this boy named Lester. I fell in love with him and, in a way, today I still am. He was married and he told me that from the beginning, but his wife had left him. He was going to get a divorce but he did not.

I went back to the institution on a parole violation. And I wasn't too happy about it. I threw my weight around, I got into trouble, and I went to the punishment cottage.

A year later I got my parole again. I was soon returned on a parole violation that was not even my fault. In fact, I was pretty stubborn about it when they had taken me back. I told the judge, "Judge, the next time you see me I'll be in the reformatory."

He said, "Oh, you're just mad right now." I said "Yes, I am mad because you took my parole away from me for no reason at all." He told me that he felt that I should have had my parole taken away. So I and some other girls escaped from there right away. We beat up two housemothers. We were soon picked up and put in jail. Well, we acted like little brats. We told them we were nineteen and twenty years old. They put us in the women's section and sent me to a psychiatric hospital. There were a lot of people that I thought a lot of—a lot of people that were good to me.

One doctor really tried to help me a lot. He was very understanding, very kind. He tried his darndest not to have me sent up here, but I knew I was going to come here anyway. Although I had lost my temper, this doctor still didn't give up on me, nor did the other doctors that were there. He told me, "There is nothing wrong with you except you have an evil temper. Someday that temper will lead you to kill somebody." Well, I didn't believe it.

Finally, I was sentenced to the women's reformatory for assault. First I was in isolation. When I got out of isolation I got into an argument with one of the big top girls there. When she saw that I wasn't afraid of her she began to like me and we became good friends.

So then, as time went on I got into an awful lot of trouble here. I was involved in breaking in and entering a locked closet, stealing cigarettes and matches and things like that. I was not granted my parole. I was very, very mean about this. I took some cleaning stuff. I really intended—I wanted to kill myself. It didn't work though, which is quite fortunate, and I'm happy about it now. Anyway, I felt that I couldn't really change even if I wanted to. I worked on the farm in the reformatory, and I loved doing that. But I just didn't get along with one of the matrons. It wasn't that she didn't like me. It was just that I wanted too much attention, so I thought I would raise hell. Then I'd go to the cell. Anyway I was granted my parole.

My mother had come up to see me and had wanted me to come home and live with her. I did, but it didn't work out. I went home, but ten days later I was kicked out of the house. My sister took me into her home. I started working in a nursing home. I had an awful lot of fun there, and I loved those patients. To me, those people that I worked for there didn't seem to be really interested in those people except for what money they brought. But these old people, they would reach out for people to love them and to try and understand them. And of course, I, being so much like them . . . actually I was attached to them. But I got fired from there, and I was quite hurt about that. I didn't try to get another job.

I moved away and things started going bad for me. I just didn't care what happened anymore. I was going to have a baby. The father of my baby and I broke up when I found out I was pregnant. I started going with another boy whom I loved very much. Deep in my heart I want to, but if I ever want to change, I guess I can't. So anyway, my friend had really gotten me upset. She said to me over the phone, "Do you want a little nigger baby running after you calling you mama?" Right then and there I decided that I was going to try to get rid of that child. I got some pills, but I thank God to this day that they didn't work. Like I have told many people, "If God wanted that baby to die he would have taken her life then when I tried to." So I felt that God had given me my little baby for some reason. I don't know what it is yet. But maybe someday I will. When I had my little baby, it was one of the happiest moments of my life. I wanted to keep it more than anything else in this world. It was the only thing I was able to cling to; my only hope of ever changing or doing something worthwhile in my life. My little baby is all I have right now, and right now it's the only thing I want. Her father got married not too long ago. Fine, if he can be happy. I have no grudges against him. But I feel this way: that my little girl is going to be brought up to the best of my ability. I don't want her to be brought up the way I was. For the simple reason that I don't want to go up and visit her behind bars, or have her cry out, "Mommy help me," when she is in trouble. So I feel that if I ever want to do something worthwhile in my life, I have to take care of my child and bring her up right, with or without a husband or a father.

I feel right now very depressed, because I've only seen my little baby once. That was the day she was baptized. But I know now that it won't be too long, and I'll see her. My little baby is my family. My family doesn't care for me. I don't let myself think of it too much, because. . . . Still, in a way, it hurts to know that your mother and father want no part of you.

I have been in institutions half my life, but my feeling is this: if and when I go out this time and I can't change, then I never will be able to. I do not want the baby to be taken away from me, because I would never try to straighten my life out again if this happened.

I find, as time goes on, that my feelings toward people in this institution are very harsh. Sometimes I even say I hate them. I admit I don't. I know these people are doing their job, but you'd think that they could reach out to each and every one of these girls. Maybe they can. Maybe they won't. I don't know. I know people with authority sometimes take advantage of it. They don't care how they enforce the rules. But the warden— I doubt if they could ever find a woman to take her place. Or to have somebody who can understand the girls with as much authority as she has. She's the kind of person who listens and doesn't butt in and say, "You should do this" or "You should do that." She waits until you are all through talking. But I feel that they should have more group therapy here, or they should have more social workers for the girls, because there is a lot of friction. A lot of the girls get upset. Now I've been here a long time. I feel that this place has helped me a great deal, and I also feel that it has hurt me a great deal. By helping me, I mean it has tried to make me more of a lady, to be more quiet, take more responsibilities. It has hurt me by denying me of the right to tell my side of the story.

I really don't think that my life story has been as good as it should have been, or has been as bad as I thought it would be or think it is. Because as I look around me I can see where girls have had more heartaches and more hurts and more disappointments than I have. There are some girls who don't have a family at all. Some don't even have children. Or some who have had children have had them taken away. We all, I guess, feel sorry for ourselves.

Doris is a sixteen-year-old Negro girl. She looks very mature, older than her age. She walks with the grace of a queen and has an unusually cultured voice and way of expressing herself. She has an almost tranquil beauty, and her features reflect sensitivity and intelligence. The following was Doris's account when she talked with the researcher alone after they had met at the breakfast table:

I think I know exactly what made difficulties for me. I developed much too fast, even physically. I menstruated at the age of nine and had the appearance of a grown woman, so I took on an adult frame of mind. I insisted that I could do what any adult could do. My mother tried to prevent this, but I was so adamant that she finally gave up and said, "You can do whatever you want to." At age fourteen I had my own apartment. I worked. I missed a lot of childhood. I have given up childhood far too early. I am the mother of two children. One of the children is four years old and the other is eighteen months. I don't know where they are. One of the girls tells me that her grandmother has one of the children. There is no point in looking for them. I had to give them up for adoption because I could not earn enough, and I should go to school. When I go to school I am always on the honor roll. After I had my second child I had no more trouble about sex.

Somehow then the childish things were coming back. I became a kid again. I liked to do the things that children do, like roller skating. Then, suddenly it all crashed down on me again. Here I am again. I was at a teenage party, and it was not bad at first. Then they started to drink, and I did not like that. I decided to leave them and go home by myself. I wish I had not done that. It would have been better that I stayed. It was 1 A.M. and I wanted to get home. A man offered me a ride, and I accepted it. The moment I was in the car he turned me over to the police. I don't know whether he was a stool pigeon or whatever it was. He swore I propositioned him. This is really not true, but nobody will believe me. I think, though, I should not feel bitter. I don't have it on my conscience. I have done other bad things though, so maybe that's what I am here for.

I have been subjected to much injustice. I have always been good-natured. I don't let it get under my skin. I am not inhuman. When I was first locked up here I thought of running away. I went on the fire escape and walked up and down thinking I would run. After I walked enough, the urge to run left me. No sense messing up my whole life. If I run, I wouldn't help myself. It makes no sense. I argued with myself against running. I told myself that I am better off where I am at this moment. This is a bad place, and I know it. Yet, I think as long as I have will power this place can't hurt me too much.

In a way I am glad that it all ended this way. I intend to finish school here. Then I want to go home and take a job to help my mother. When I got up here, her ADC [Aid to Dependent Children] was cut off, and the same thing happened when I left her before. I owe her that to take care of her. My mother has always done things for me. She is still young and has a heart condition and has a bad back. I worry about her. As long as my mother lives I want to be near her. She is too lonesome. I had tried to talk her into remarriage, but she won't do it. It is my fault that she aged. I must make it up to her. She was a pretty young woman when I had my first baby, and she got gray hair.

I don't want to kill my mother. I am guilty, because I let her down.

My father died when I was one year old. My stepfather adopted me—that's why I have his name—he also died after a few years. He upset my mother terribly, because he was a bigamist, and she had not known it. This went on and on—all this wrangling—and I just did not care for her at that time.

Mother had to go out and work after this, and I was in a big house all alone. I did baby sitting, and the welfare arranged for me to take care of elderly ladies, but I was too lonely. I hung around street corners. But it was all my fault what happened to me, not hers. She had to work.

When I first was here I felt so bad, I fussed at everybody. I constantly used profane language until I told myself that it must stop. I got along much better in this cottage. Here I know girls from school and from the outside. Here we understand each other. You wondered about my diction and language. You see, on the outside some of us have a private language. It is full of ugly words and jive. In school I studied poetry. I somehow felt that I wanted this to be a part of my language. Jive seemed to be out of place. We read *Macbeth*, and I loved it. I learned words and expressions from literature. I like to get hold of good literature. In school they suggested to us to write sonnets, and I wrote them on assignments. It seems like you can express a lot in this.

But you know, that poses a problem. What should one write about in a poem? Why should one write about bad things? You can't write about sad and bad things, because you don't want others to be sad and bad. And yet what can I write? You can't just write about the truth. Some things I don't feel about—I just don't *feel!* I want to write, and I don't know how to do it without making people sad.

I don't want to be married. I don't want to settle down. I want to travel and see things. I want to be able to tell my children the good things I have done when I was young, and the interesting things that I have seen. I don't want to get married and have to tell them only that I have been in an institution in my youth.

I guess I would like to study. But for the near future, I think of becoming a good secretary and stenographer. I have skills. I have learned how to run an IBM machine, I am taking typing and stenography. I can fix hair very well and I have my Junior Red Cross certificate. I have training in many things. I must be able to make a living.

I have done many bad things in my life that they don't know about. I am here for something I haven't done. Maybe this is justice. This cottage is not bad, so I am not so worried here. My probation officer wanted me to tell her more about the man who had lied about me. I don't care to talk about him anymore. If they want to get ahold of him, they must find him. I do not care to hound the man. He did me a great deal of wrong, but it will not be better by hounding him. I want to thank you for talking with me. You say you cannot help us, but it helps simply to talk to someone who listens.

Mary is a slender seventeen-year-old Indian girl. Her clothing indicates more poverty than those of other girls. She was burning to talk. Her account which follows was once interrupted because she had to go to school but she asked to return and to continue. Mary wanted her account to be tape-recorded. There was an intense desire to make herself understood.

When I was five years old my mother sent me to the first institution. I was there for one year, but I never knew why they sent me there. They simply sent me there quite suddenly. I think it was because my parents didn't get along, and they wanted to get rid of us kids. She says that she wanted us to learn something, but I don't believe it. I was so terribly scared, because I couldn't understand why I was away. I never had anything—no clothing, no shoes. I was *so* scared. I stole crayons in school just because I was too scared to ask for something. My dad was terribly mean. He was drunk all the time, and the moment he came through the door he beat me up. I got it across the face for nothing, just standing there. I was beat up every day until I was twelve years old. My sister was so afraid of my father! When he came into the house, she just shook and she wet her pants.

When I was seven years old my uncle and aunt took me with them. They traveled all the time. They swore at each other and at me. They called me a brat.

I went to school with Sisters. For the first time I prayed, and I liked that. But I was no good at school. I never had any breakfast at home. In fact, I had nothing to eat. I never had any clean clothes. I was so ashamed! We never had meals. We were too scared to talk to anybody.

I never had any religion. I hold that against my parents. I probably should forgive them, but I just can't.

Then after all that, the welfare put us in a foster home. I liked it there, but my sister didn't. It was the first time in my life that I had real meals and that I got a birthday cake.

But then my mother came and got us again. The welfare should not allow that. My dad whipped me fiercely. One day I had diarrhea and couldn't walk to the bathroom. He got so mad at me he threw a fork at me and it hit my chin. He whipped my ear, and I still have a scar on it.

I had for the first time my period, and I had no idea what it meant. I was so scared, but I couldn't talk. My mother didn't tell me. When she saw it, she just gave me a pad and said that I would always have it. I thought I was terribly sick.

Before that I once had pneumonia. My mother and dad were not at home. I didn't want to go to the hospital. I wanted to take care of the younger children. I always tried to fix something to eat for them, but I hardly knew how. I finally had to go to the hospital. And then I got into the foster home. That was a nice woman. She treated me nicely but I could not speak to her. I didn't know how to speak to anybody. I never asked her about the period either. I didn't know that other girls had it or that she had it. I only knew that my mother and I had it. In that foster home I was kind of happy, but I ran away. Both my sister and I ran away. I think it was because we had to do a lot of work. We ran around, but we had nothing to eat so we turned ourselves in. We went to the police.

I got into the Home. I just *loved* it there. I only wish they had not released me when they did. You see, I still didn't know anything about the facts of life. The girls talked about "fixes" and about "Sharpies" and about smoking. I just heard about the fun. I just didn't know what it meant. I didn't know anything about the facts of life. I never asked anybody there, because I didn't feel like . . . I just didn't want . . . I thought I'd be ridiculing myself by asking somebody. You know how you feel when you ask a silly question? I thought it would be that silly that somebody would laugh at me. We didn't have a social worker or a housemother. We had a Sister, but I didn't want to talk about things like that with her. I just let it ride by. I never knew Sisters knew things like that. I thought they were just holy. But they do know things like that, because it's important in their lives too. I never did tell anybody. Really, I don't think I've ever had the chance to talk to anybody about things like that.

I was there almost two years. In all this time my mother wrote me three times—three times! My eldest brother wrote to me and said that he would want to make a home for me. He thought maybe we could be a family. I wrote to my dad that I forgave him, but he never answered, and I still have hard feelings.

My mother took me back home, and I started going with boys. First I went with a young boy who was nice. It's embarrassing to talk about it, but I just didn't understand it. They boasted that they had stolen a car. I had overheard it. I never had thought of liquor. I hated it. Other girls talked about boys and liquor and I didn't understand it. One day I was at a Sunday picnic and they offered me beer. My little sister offered it to me. I said I didn't want it, but she said I was chicken. That's what you don't want to hear. I drank it, and I got high. Boy, did I get high! For three days I did nothing but get high and raise cain! Sometimes when you do something wrong you feel guilty. When you're drinking you don't even care. That's the difference between being drunk and being sober. I was only fifteen or sixteen years old when I was getting drunk. Then the floor was way wide, the ceiling way high. Everything looked different. It was funny. Now when I drink it isn't a happy feeling. When I'm drinking now, I'm just drunk. When I get drunk now I don't feel good or anything like that. But I still feel like I can do anything I want to without caring. It makes me more courageous. I've gotten into fights with other girls. I had to drink in order to get into a fight, you know. I have to have alcohol to give me the strength and courage to be able to do that, see?

I started going with younger boys, then older boys. Then from older boys I went to men. I got involved with this one kid. He was about eighteen at the time; I was fifteen then. I used to hang around with his sister. We used to have a crowd. I didn't know anything about sex, I didn't know what it was really like. So we had sexual relations. I knew it was wrong. I knew it was a sin. I didn't know how come men did it, and I didn't know they got pleasure out of it or anything. I didn't know that you could get pregnant by that either. Here I was fifteen years old, and I didn't even know that stuff! Then after that my older sister and I got to talking lady-to-lady like, and she told me things. She was the one who told me how girls get pregnant.

I didn't like school. They sent me to school in the city. It was more complicated than it was in an institution. I didn't like school. I tried, but evidently I didn't try hard enough to accomplish anything. I skipped school, started playing hooky. I started staying at these boys' places and drinking, and I learned how to smoke. We used to call the school and tell them that we were the boy's mother and to excuse him from school. Then we'd say this was my mother and to excuse me from school. We'd make up excuses for each other. Then they found out that I was playing hooky. They called home one time, and my mother was home and I wasn't at home. They said I wasn't at school, and they were wondering why. When I came home after school was out and had come home for supper, mother said, "You've been playing hooky, haven't you?" I said, "Yes," and that I didn't want to go to school now. I said I didn't like it. I didn't have nice clothes. If I wanted anything nice for school, I had to go to work on Saturdays and do day work. Then I had to go to a rummage sale to buy some clothes. I don't believe that my mother ever did buy any school clothes for me.

My father wasn't at home. My mother and he got divorced. Mother got married again. She and the stepfather used to drink and fight all the time. I never dared to get involved with my mother's and dad's fights. But, because I felt I wanted to help her, I always got myself into my stepdad's and mother's fights. I didn't want him to do what my dad did to my mother. So I'd get involved. I'd say, "Leave her alone . . . or I'll help you fight." I pulled her away or knocked him down or something, hit him on the head with a beer bottle or with a chair. I hid her in my room. After that he didn't like me, so he kicked me out. He told me to "Get out! Go on! I don't want anything to do with you! You're no good anyway!" So I took off. I was going with this one boy. We were engaged and were going to get married, but my mother didn't like it. She didn't want me to get married to him. So I thought, "Maybe if I'd get pregnant she'd let me get married." But I couldn't get pregnant. He went into the service and I started going around with other boys.

After that we'd go around town, hang around bowling alleys, hang around theaters. I was going out to parties with boys and girls, smoking and drinking and trying out new stuff . . . like smoking aspirins. If we didn't have anything to drink, we'd smoke aspirins in cigarettes or else put aspirins into our pop and drink it. Then one time we got hold of this kid who was selling marijuana and we got hold of some of that and tried that. We got involved in things like that. I don't know whatever made me do it. It's just the fact that everybody else is doing it, so why shouldn't I do it?

Then I met another guy I kinda liked and fell in love with him—or what you call falling in love. So I stayed with him for a couple of months, and I really did care for him very much, except he drank too much. I didn't drink too much then. I did once in a while, but I didn't drink in a bar. So then I got pregnant. We were staying at his sister's because I didn't have any place to go, because I was kicked out at home. So, I don't know how we broke apart, It was in the summertime when we broke up. We went to a party and he was talking to this girl and I got jealous. So he took off with the girl. So I took off. I didn't know I was pregnant yet then. I packed up my clothes and took off for home. I asked my mother if I could come home again and she said yes. She had broke up with my stepdad. So I figured everything would be all right. I told her I was ready to settle down. I was sixteen years old and I got a job with a club doing dishes. I was making a dollar an hour. My mother, at that time, didn't know I was pregnant. I didn't tell her until I started getting sick in the morning. Then I knew, because my sister had told me things like that. I didn't want my mother to know, because I thought maybe she'd condemn me for it. So I was working at the club and I'd get sick. And I didn't eat breakfast then. And you know, when you're preganant you have to eat breakfast, you have to. It's necessary. I didn't eat breakfast, and I went to grab a glass of milk and down it, and it all came up again. My mother saw that, and she said, "Are you sick or something?" I said, "I must have drunk it too fast." But that evening I told her that I was pregnant. So she told me to leave the house.

I went to the welfare office, and they asked me who I was pregnant by, but I didn't tell them. So I stayed with my sister then. The boy I got pregnant by came to see me a couple of times. We planned on getting married, but then I backed out because I didn't want to get married. I figured he didn't work. Then, if we got married he wouldn't be able to take care of us. He kept on seeing me. He'd come up to the place drunk and try to get into my room so I had to move. So, I ran away. I had to quit my job, too. I got myself a place in a hotel and stayed there. I managed for two weeks to get along on my own. So when it came time for me to have my baby I went to the hospital. It was about two weeks early and it was stillborn. It was a little girl. I asked them to baptize it. I wanted that baby real bad. I had intentions to keep it. I think anybody that would have a child would want to keep it. But I lost it. I didn't want to go back to my boyfriend. I didn't want to have anything to do with him, because I was sick, I was sick in my heart. I figured that if I stayed away from him, maybe I'd be okay. So I tried to stay away from him, but he bothered me. My sister and mother and me were quarreling all the time. After I had my baby they were calling me bad names and called me down for being pregnant. Of course, I wasn't the only one that had illegitimate children. My older sister is my half sister and my sister's kids are . . . some of them are illegitimate. They were calling me names, but then I didn't want to call them any names either, because it wasn't right. I felt sorry for about three months after I had my baby. I had my baby in May.

In July I got picked up for being drunk. I started drinking extensively. My boyfriend kept on trying to get back to me. And I had to get away from him all the time. I was drinking with him, and we were talking, and we got into a big quarrel, and the cops told me I was drunk. We were quarreling in the middle of the street. He wanted to take me to a hotel and I didn't want to go. So I told the police I was only fourteen years old. I was sixteen, and I told them I was fourteen. So they picked me up, and they let him go. I got put on probation, and I got to stay with my aunt and uncle in the South.

The environment wasn't what I thought it would be. It's so different down there that I didn't like it. The people, the way they talk, and they act. Prejudice about colored people. When I'd talk to colored people, or if I had any interest in boys at all, my aunt called me down because she knew I'd had that baby. Every time I went out for a couple of hours they'd think maybe I was going out and having sexual relations. When I did go out, it was either because I went out and walked to think about what I wanted to do—that was my reasons for going. One time I was gone for three hours. I was mad at my aunt, and I was gone for three hours. I walked around, and when I came back my uncle asked me where I was, and I told him that I was downtown. He didn't believe me. He asked me if I got drunk and just sobered off and I said, "No." They thought that I was.

We were trying to find me a job. I didn't want to go back to school because I hated school. I just despised it. What made me hate school was the fact that I didn't have good clothes, nice sharp clothes like some of the girls had. What clothes I did have weren't the right kind of clothes. They were different; you wouldn't wear them to school. Some kids wear brand new clothes. Then they'd keep them nice and all the time have nice clothes to wear to school. But I didn't have that. That's what I hated about going to school. I was too scared to talk to girls. I think the girls weren't my type. The only ones who talked to me were girls who had been in trouble also. One girl invited me to her place, but she was just as bad as I. She liked to go with boys and drink and steal. She had everything she wanted, but she stole.

I got mad one day and packed up and left. I was on probation. I packed up my suitcase and I left. I told them that I wanted to get out of there. The night before that I stayed out until two or three o'clock in the morning. I had met this soldier boy, and he was just nice to me. We were talking about his mother and my mother, and his mother was part Indian. He was real nice to me. We just talked. We went to a movie. We went to have something to eat, then sat in the park and talked, talked about our lives. I told him my troubles, and I told him what I used to be and everything. I got so involved in telling him because he was so nice. I just knew he understood everything I said. I told him I didn't know if I'd ever get married and he just laughed at me. He said, "Oh, you'll get married one of these days. Somebody will want you." I said, "Oh yeah?" He said, "You're young, you've made mistakes when you were young, you didn't know what was going on. You'll find a good guy who will understand." I asked him if he understood. . . . I did want companionship, you know, and to be able to talk to him.

It got so late that he walked me part way home. We were just talking, and we forgot about the time. But my uncle thought I was busy in bed or something. And I don't blame him, because I was out late. You can try to explain, but they know it all. That's how I happened to get to the delinquency institution.

I don't know if I could ever forget about my past, but there are things that I am worried about, and things that I can't forget that I'm worried about. I want to get married. Everybody wants to, every woman wants to. But with the life that I've had, and the past that I've had, I'll have to go far away to find a husband. How am I going to explain to him my life? Sometimes if you tell men things they'll take advantage of you. You know, if I knew things that I know now. . . . Oh, I don't know, I wouldn't have done the things. See? It's just like with sex-life. Sex-life can ruin a person for a good marriage and a good life. I think that a woman should keep herself preserved for a man whom you love. How am I going to find myself a good man in life with the life I've had? I'll never be able to find a good man. I hope to go out on my own and take care of myself. I don't want anybody to support me. I will have to support myself sooner or later. I'll probably have to be washing dishes or something now until I finish high school, but I do want to finish high school.

When I get out of here I hope to get myself a job and get myself a place to stay, get myself a cute little apartment, a kitchen, and a bedroom and a front room. I'd like to get myself a lot of nice clothes that I can work in. I'd like to be able to get some nice clothes so I can go to school, night school. There are so many things that I'd like to do, but the most important thing I'd like to do is be a nurse's aide because I've taken care of people before. I have taken some nurse's aide training here. But I haven't finished the course because I ran away from here. It's going to be hard, if I do do it. City life could easily drag me into being the same old thing, and I don't want to be that. I want to be able to go out and find a good man and get married. I want to have a lot of kids. I hope that I won't get married until I'm about twenty-four, because I've wasted a lot of my young life.

I'm here for drinking and having had such a crooked life. And whose fault is it? It's my fault for being so ignorant. I think that's what I'd call it—being ignorant. I blame some of it on my mother, because I think mothers should always tell their daughters about the facts of life. One time she told me, "I'd like to see you get married in white." I didn't know what she meant; I didn't know she meant being a virgin. I blame her, and I blame my father. The first time we were taken away from them they should have just kept us in a foster home and left us there and not give us back. Yes, I did want to go back because I figured that she was my mother, and I wanted to be with my mother. I don't know her very well. I don't know my father very well; I don't know his habits, because I've never lived with him long enough. You have to know your mother in order to be happy. There is such a thing as to be with your mother to be happy, and another, to be with your mother because she's your mother. I didn't care about happiness or sorrow or whatever it was. I just wanted to be with my mother.

There are other girls here like me. There are girls who have had the same life as I have; who have walked the same road as I have and have had the same kind of folks as I have. Their whole life is just like mine. The only thing, they take it differently. We all take things differently. I take mine hard, because I figure, "Well, why did these things have to happen? They could have been prevented! They could have!" My life has been a lot of sorrow. I've been through a lot of things in my life— hard things to take. To me, the Depression couldn't have been anything like when my dad used to beat me. When you run away you run from the sorrow that you have inside you. I mean you feel sorry for yourself because you don't get what some girls get, like letters from home. I think my main problem is looking for love, or trying to get someone to love me. Sometimes I would give my mother money, and still she wouldn't do anything. No, what I want to do is take care of myself. I don't want to depend on anybody except myself.

You see, this is my whole life. The whats and why, I don't know. I told you about everything, didn't I?

Bea, seventeen years old, looked like a typical teenager with her dark hair piled high on the top of her head in the hair style then fashionable, in skirt and blouse and loafers. Yet Bea could also look twenty years older when she got dressed up, put on high heels, and wore the kind of sophisticated dress she loved. She was exceedingly verbal, talking rapidly and sounding as if she were out of breath. She expressed herself without hesitation during the first contact with the researcher:

I am here a long time. I think I stayed too long. One can stay here far too long. I learned a lot from the girls when I got here, when I was thirteen years old. First I was only skipping school and stayed out, but then I learned a lot more what to do.

I have a good family, but it is a boring family. I wanted to see something. I wanted excitement. What do I mean by excitement? I want to see bright lights and night life. I ran to New York, and I like to do things that go on other people's nerves. Why? Well, they always think *they* know. The adults always think they always know everything better than we do. I want to show them that I know something too. If they know so much, maybe I should learn fast. They always say we are not old enough. I thought, "I will show them—that I am old enough. I can take care of myself." They always babied me. I hate to be babied. Why can I not stay out as long as I want to? I think I know what I want. They don't, certainly. I never thought what heartache I produced. I know that now, but I still am wild.

When I got out of the institution, I got involved with the girls I knew from it. That is violation, but these are my friends! I knew it was violation, but I thought I could get by with it. I went to a beauty school, but I dropped out of there. I didn't want a job. I slept during the day, and then I got up at 5 P.M., and then I left. I went with older boys. I like older boys better than the young ones. When we are together we dance and drink. I even smoked reefers. Oh, you feel like in the clouds! You ought to try it sometime! Everything is so nice when you do it! I am not yet addicted to it, so it doesn't hurt me that I don't have it here.

I am not used to a regular life. I am not really interested in any job. I guess I was born that way. When I was little I liked to throw rocks at people and then run. I am the only one who is that way in the family. There are four of us. One brother is in the army. Two of my sisters are married. I was the baby, but I hate to be a baby. Everybody tells me what to do. Sometimes I pout if I don't get my way.

I am crazy about clothes. My parents can afford to give me clothes. My father has a good job.

I love to sew. I just like to do it. . . . No, nobody taught it to me. I just picked it up, and I can sew any dress I want to sew. I design dresses. Boy, how I wish to work with clothes. . . . You mean one can do that without having gone to college? I never knew that. Boy, if somebody would find *that* for me!

I am now a senior. I will graduate when I am here. I like school now, but I don't know for how long. What I like is sewing, art, woodcraft, and modern problems. The modern problems I like best are family problems, not so much political stuff.

What I want in life? I wish I could be nice, would have a job and stay home and later travel. It's hard to find a job. If I could just do some dress designing, fix up furniture. I want to be married and have two children. I want to be married to a well-to-do old man who has lots of money. I really can't love old men, but I'd rather have the money. I like money.

Whether I have ever been in love? I have, really! In fact, he even came before me, and that is real love. He was working. His grandfather is part colored, and that was a problem with my family. Do you think that is right? What is all that reason for all the prejudice?

People are prejudiced everywhere. They are even prejudiced here. Maybe not the people in the office, but the housemothers are. I tell you I have heard them call a girl "dirty Indian" or "nigger." How can we respect people like that?

Sure I wish I could fall in love with somebody I could love *and* who has money; but if I have to choose, I would choose money. I want someone who gets somewhere. I would work during the first year of marriage or perhaps in a long engagement. I don't want to have children right away. Children should have a good life and should not be pushed around.

How I would raise my children? I think they must learn for themselves. I ran away from home to find out things for myself.

Parents can't tell you. I always have to find out things for myself.

I seldom believe another person. I don't trust them. No, it's not because they lied to me, but I have always lied to people. I can lie without the other one ever knowing it. How can I believe people when I know how easy it is to lie? I lie because I hate nagging and hollering. I always lie to protect myself.

This life in an institution hardens you, and you end up with a complex about yourself. I mean you think, "I am no good like anyone else. There's no use trying. You're just crazy." I know I am not crazy, but I need to talk to someone who understands and who doesn't think I am crazy. And we need help on the outside, not only here. People don't even look at you as a real girl when you get out of here.

When I was little I belonged to some clubs . . . and I was with the Bluebirds. I liked grade school so much better, but then we moved to another neighborhood, and I didn't like it. I always went back to my old neighborhood, and the trouble started. I spent nights in jail. It's so filthy. You learn a lot.

Sometimes I write poetry.

You have heard the differences in life histories, in economic background, in feelings. These are only a small sample of the girls I saw. They dwelt mostly on their problems—it could not be otherwise, for they spoke while being held in closed institutions and under the impact of beginning to look into themselves. It is important to add that they also knew laughter and jokes, that some wrote beautiful poetry. Bertha sewed and knitted in her cell for her child. Bea made costumes for Halloween. Mary enjoyed doing household tasks, especially when the record player was on full blast—like any teenager, but in her own way.

What, then, can be learned about the girl in conflict? What will give the key to better understanding?

3. LONELINESS IN AN ANONYMOUS WORLD

*"For in its innermost depths,
youth is lonelier than old age."* [1]

When Anne Frank wrote this, she was separated from her friends, surrounded by a hostile world, but she lived with her family, a loving and caring one. Why is loneliness such a strong theme in the diary of this fifteen-year-old? Can it be explained only by the special circumstances under which she lived? Was she right that youth in general feel so alone, more so than people at any other age?

Any human being at one time or another in his life recognizes the recurring loneliness in which he lives. Somehow or other, each individual has to come to terms with it. The most fortunate one finds another person with whom he or she can share his innermost thoughts, his doubts, his fears, and his joys. Such a relationship is precious. Yet even the closest relationship can never completely eliminate the occasional feeling of being alone, of carrying the burden of one's essential humanness.

Many less fortunate ones never find the one close mate or friend, but become part of the lives of several others by exchanging ideas, thoughts, and feelings in intellectual or social interchange. Every person, at all age periods, needs communication with others. Interdependence is essential to human survival from the cradle to the grave. In the lifeless hands of an older woman who had committed

---

[1] Anne Frank, *The Diary of a Young Girl* (New York: The Modern Library, 1952), p. 278.

suicide was a little slip of paper with the notation, "Man does not live by bread alone, but by faith, by admiration, by sympathy." [2]

The human being is always in transition, always developing, always in need of others. But the most vulnerable stages of his development are those in which he is totally dependent on his human environment. A small child cannot survive physically unless others care for him. The infant cannot talk about his feelings of loneliness, but without warm human support he does not develop and can survive only precariously.[3] And when physical faculties disappear or diminish, as in old age, real dependency appears again.

On the surface, adolescence does not have this attribute. On the contrary, it is the period of life where the youngster emerges from childhood and begins to assert his independence. He can, if need be, stand on his own feet, even in our times. He will not perish without adult nurture. Adolescent rebellion—and its drive toward independence—is known and accepted as necessary for all young people who must move into the tasks of adulthood and mainte-nance of relationship to their own generation. The girls I saw often expressed this rebellion. Yet the angry cry of "I'm old enough, why don't they let me do what I want to?" was almost always accom-panied—and sometimes even drowned out—by "There's nobody I can talk to, they don't understand." Or "One expects parents to listen. Why don't they?" Or "I need friends. They tell me not to meet with the same girls I met here in the institution, but I can't be alone, and how can I find others?" Or "I felt so lonely. When I was in his arms, it was the only time I wasn't afraid."

It seemed to be especially painful for the girls to move out of childhood where it was legitimate to be dependent. Even those girls who had no protecting, loving parents and who were exposed early to the harsh demand of caring for themselves, experienced—at least during the early years of childhood—a certain exemption from personal responsibility, through a general attitude of society that someone *should* care for them. It is not accidental that most of the girls said, "The trouble started when I was twelve or thirteen." It started *when it was no longer legitimate for them to be depend-ent* as children. As many girls expressing a common feeling ex-claimed:

[2] Ralph Waldo Emerson in his *Lectures and Biographical Sketch.*

[3] See René A. Spitz, "Hospitalism: An Inquiry into the Genesis of Psychiatric Conditions in Early Childhood," in *Psychoanalytic Study of the Child* (New York: International Universities Press, 1945), I, 53-74; "Hospitalism: A Follow-up Report," *loc. cit.* (1946), II, 113-17.

I wish I were a child! People don't understand. Adults forget. I was twelve years old when I got into trouble. . . . I ran away ten times; I was homesick. Nothing keeps me when I am homesick. . . . Oh, *I wish I were a child!*

Each generation is really not so different from another. It is only that adults sometimes forget that. . . . One doesn't talk much with parents. Perhaps people never did, *but today one expects it more.* One should be able to.

Have you ever been lonely? When I was in the foster home I could not see my sister or my brother. I felt so lonely. I wanted to hang around other kids.

I am just terribly lonesome. I don't think I was even in love. I just wanted to get close because I was so lonesome. I wouldn't marry him. I was aware I could have a child.

I wish I could get help. If I could go to a club where there are real friends! Real friends understand you. It all revolves around friendship. I would like to have an older friend. I have one and she is a woman who works, but my mother doesn't like me to go to her. But I need friends.

I like to meet new people, but I haven't many friends. I thought the girls were my friends, but they really are my enemies. They talk behind your back. I want friends so badly that I always push myself on others.

It is part of the characteristic quality of adolescence to be intro-spective, to feel misunderstood, to search for friends among con-temporaries. The old adult world must be partially left behind. Companions of the same age allow for experimentation with ideas, with the beginning adventure into a new adult world. Other young-sters can give support and provide something like a mirror for one to find out who he is, whether he is similar to or different from others. The literature has been filled in recent years with the need of adolescents—boys and girls alike—to search for identity. This need grows out of a loss of security. What I found in the girl in conflict was something beyond this: loneliness accompanied by despair. The desperation of loneliness was based on a feeling of being unprotected, being incapable of making and finding friends, being surrounded by an anonymous and powerful adult world.

Adolescent boys, too, often feel lonely and search for understand-ing and friends. Yet, in general, this does not seem to be the central core of their problems, not their most outspoken ache. While these girls also strive for independence, their need for *dependence* is unusually great—and almost completely overlooked and unfulfilled. This need for support seems to exist in all adolescent girls, but the frustration and actual despair are stronger in most of those adjudicated delinquent. They yearn for friendship but seem to have little capacity for it. The unfulfilled need for dependence makes them feel exceedingly lonely, but they do not know camaraderie. The touchstone of our understanding of the adolescent girl in conflict is not just loneliness, it is loneliness which sees no way out, an inner helplessness confronted with an enveloping "anonymous" world. People are rarely people: they are "Court," "Church," "School," even "Adult," but rarely father, mother, teacher, helper, friend.

The delinquent girl suffers, like many boys, from lack of opportunity, from lack of success. But her drive toward success is never separated from her need for people, for interpersonal involvement. An intelligent thirteen-year-old, full of rebellious spirit, lagging behind in school in spite of her desire to study and go to the university, underlines this: "I would like to share an apartment with friends. I mean *real* friends, not just to have the rent cheaper."

What are the reasons for this essential loneliness in the girl? Some will be found in the nature of being an adolescent *girl,* in her biological makeup and her particular position in our culture and time; other reasons will lie in the environment—both physical and human—in which many girls who get into serious conflict live.

Meaning of Physical Maturity

The move into adolescence is signified for the girl by a definite and dramatic biological event, the beginning of menstruation. While physical changes in the adolescent boy also may seem strange and frightening to him, they do not call to mind injury and sickness as do those in the girl. Bleeding has the connotation of being hurt. Every modern explanation of menstruation stresses its naturalness, the possibility of absence of pain, the opportunity for girls to live an active and normal life even during the menstrual period. Yet it must be said that this thinking is by no means widespread, that ignorance and poor preparation for the bodily change in the adolescent girl is appalling. Remember the seventeen-year-old who said, "I had my period for the first time and I had no idea what it meant. I was so scared, but I couldn't ask. My mother didn't tell me.

When she saw it, she just gave me a pad. She said that I would always have it. I thought I was terribly sick."

This was no rare exception. Girls from many different backgrounds, Caucasian, Negro, and Indian alike, told about their being totally unprepared for their menstrual periods and about the resulting fear and confusion.

> I was ten years old when I got my periods. I did not know anything. I started in school. I came home from school and I was scared. I told my grandmother I was bleeding and I did not know what was wrong. She gave me a pad and told me to put it on. She did not say anything else. Later mother explained it happened to every girl and that if it didn't, I could not have a baby. I was supposed to watch myself. That's all that was explained to me. Later on, I found out from talking to other people—an aunt and an older cousin—what it was really all about, but otherwise I did not know anything about it.

> I learned all about sex education on my own. I had to find out the facts of life from my girlfriends or what I heard; I had to put two and two together. The only thing my mother said to me when I got my periods when I was nine was, "Now you are able to have babies, so be careful what you do, especially when you go out with boys."

> My mother never talked to me about sex and I remember when I got my period, she never even told me what it was. She tried to tell my sister and me at the same time. I was probably ready then, but my sister was not quite ready and it did not quite work out. My sister and I are just a year apart. When I did get my periods, I thought I was dying or something.

A 16-year-old said:

> Until two years ago, I knew absolutely nothing about sex. My mother never explained anything to me. Everything I knew and learned, I learned finally from the baby's father. He explained to me sex and menstruation and all these things.

Over and over girls talked about the beginning of puberty as something unexpected, frightening, unexplained. Information was usually gained from other youngsters, and sometimes in school, but the damage was done: fear had become part of growing up. Certainly this shock can be avoided. A happy young woman recalled the onset of biological change in her sister:

My younger sister told me that she had started to menstruate. She certainly had known about me long before that time. We always had been very close to each other. I embraced her with joy and said, "How wonderful. Now you are one of us. A little woman." Then we both told mother and she was happy too and gave her a kiss.

In this case the dependency need, the need for reassurance, and the need for being important were fulfilled. The girl felt that menstruation actually signified a positive entrance into the adult world.

The possibility of pregnancy—not just the actual fact of being pregnant—adds to the girl's greater need for protection and support, and her feelings of isolation and desertion when they are not forthcoming. All adolescents in our society, boys and girls alike, struggle with the problem of being physically mature while being expected to postpone the adult fulfillment of their sexual drives. Yet if the boy engages in sexual activity, his body does not change. The girl is confronted with the possibility of becoming pregnant. Pregnancy produces both physical and emotional changes which place on her directly the responsibility for another human being. For the girl, the consequences of sexual activity, regardless of the penalties society adds, are great, simply by virtue of the fact that she is a woman.

All through life, through all ages from birth to death, the human being evolves his personality out of a conflict between his own impulses and the demands, interests, and concerns of other people and the society around him. Maturing at any stage of development means working through such conflicts. For the adolescent girl one of the harshest tasks is placed upon her during adolescence. During a time when biological drives are especially strong and new, when they ask for experimentation and learning, they involve responsibility, often beyond the emotional, physical, or social capacity of the youngster.

The Particular Psychological Development of Girls Contributing to Loneliness

Dynamic psychology has found evidence that every young child goes through a period of special attachment to the parent of the opposite sex. Later the child begins to separate himself from this relationship in order to identify closer with the adult of his own sex. This means that the very young boy feels especially close to mother but, in growing up, will tend to become more like the father, will want to be a man. There are struggles for every child in the course of this development. The girl's development is more complicated than the boy's.[4] The boy starts out close to the parent of the opposite sex and then must identify with the one of his own sex. The girl does not start out with a relationship to the parent of the opposite sex. She starts out, just like the boy, with mother as her protector and closest love object. She must learn to direct her love to father and yet continue to identify with the original love object. While the boy, if his is a healthy development, can retain a certain form of love and affection for mother without being confused in his *identification* with the father, the girl must learn to identify with the same person who also was the first love object. Where there are healthy, warm, and giving relationships, where there is little conflict between the parents, this is not an unsurmountable task, but its subtly complicated process persists. Perhaps because of—or as part of—this struggle the girl's loneliness is intensified. She does not quite dare to make mother the confidante because, inside herself, she feels she must become like mother and yet at the same time be different from her.

Another aspect of the parent-child relationship is mother-daughter *competition* which must be recognized and worked through in adolescence. In a culture where women's significance is frequently bound to their being young and of child-bearing age, mothers want their daughters to reach this goal; at the same time, the simple fact that the daughters are growing up detracts from the mothers' own youth, their own desirability, and their own importance. Surely, there is also the possibility of competition between father and son. The literature is full of such conflicts and of presentations of the older man who competes with the young one.[5] The competition between mother and daughter is either less recognized or else is almost a taboo subject. It seems not to fit into the stereotype of the giving and understanding mother. Yet such competition can be handled or prevented only if it is recognized as a normal possible occurrence at least in our culture. It must be repeated that these conflicts are possible and inherent in the relationship between all mothers and daughters, but they do not necessarily lead to disturb-

---

[4] Peter Blos, *On Adolescence* (New York: Free Press of Glencoe, Inc., 1962).

[5] For instance, see John Steinbeck, *East of Eden* (New York: The Viking Press, Inc., 1952).

ance or delinquency. They are there, like our lungs and stomachs and brains, but they become painful or diseased only when other factors are added.

Most adolescents find it difficult to admit their dependency, especially to the people close to them. There is a certain pride in and yearning for not being a child anymore. There is an overwhelming feeling of not being understood, especially by the people who knew them as children. The moments when an adolescent will admit his fears to a father or mother are rare and signify an unusually good relationship. William Saroyan expresses this through the young boy who is proud to have a job for the first time and who cherishes his independence, but who turns in an hour of despair to his mother and says, "I'm lonely and I don't know what I'm lonely for. . . . Everything is changed, but don't let it change too much for *us*." [6]

To this particular adolescent the mother is still available as a secure, steady protection in his present turmoil. The adult, especially the parent, is someone the adolescent needs to rely on—even if he or she fights the adult. Most of the youngsters I met had no communication with adults, especially not with their parents. There was an inseparable gulf, a feeling that there was no understanding. It went beyond the normal separation of two generations. It left them alone, frightened, angry, or desperate.

The Image of the Adult

To many delinquent girls whom I met, the image of the adult was a person who was:

1. brutal (especially men)
2. ineffectual and vascillating (especially women)
3. "phony," a hypocrite
4. an anonymous authority.

These images were based frequently on actual experiences with adults, experiences so severe that one marvels at the resilience of the human spirit and emotions which made it possible for these girls to continue functioning and, surprisingly, to still search for

[6] William Saroyan, *The Human Comedy* (New York: Harcourt, Brace & World, Inc., 1944), p. 34.

different relationships with adults. Certainly some had become so immune that the word "trust" had no meaning to them and the basic intent of their lives was either self-destruction or revenge, either of which took on a variety of forms in behavior.

Self-destruction may become actual suicide, or it may be expressed in excessive drinking—a "forgetting" of existence, a move into stupor. Girls took alcohol more for this purpose than for stimulation. In fact, some girls spoke with distress about the fact that drinking heightened their consciousness of being alive; this was the reason they did not care for it. Such girls then looked around for other drugs—depressants, not stimulants. They wanted to be *away* from everything.

Revenge was most frequently expressed in general rebellion, in flaunting the mores of the adult world, sometimes taking the form of stealing. Interestingly enough, in a group of my college students who were asked to describe some of their past delinquent acts— usually undetected—the revenge motive for stealing was outstanding. If they felt their employers paid too small wages, they felt justified in stealing in order to get even with them.

All adolescents go through a period of some rebellion, of questioning the authority of adults, of feeling either misunderstood or not understood at all. At that age the bridge between the two generations is always a rather precarious one. But the picture of the adult in general is not so hard or so remote as it is in the mind of the girl in harsh conflict with society. The girls who were unmarried mothers, and who were not considered delinquent, expressed their feelings in the normal adolescent ambivalence toward adults:

> Adults don't understand what you have to go through. . . . It is easier to talk with the girls. They are in the same boat. They understand better.

There is the identification with other youngsters, disappointment, but no hatred of the adult.

> The only one I feel close to and trust now is my Dad. He calls me every day. He cries when he says he loves me. That hurts me. I don't want to hurt him again. He means so much to me. He had a hard life.

Here is warmth and trust, though some exclusion of others: *"The only one . . . ."*

I have never been able to talk to my parents until now. Now we are a lot closer, and they are more interested. Yet it is still very difficult to talk with mother. Dad is easier to talk to.

Something in the relationship of parents and youngsters allowed for communication though it had been interrupted. Each parent is perceived as a person.

I don't get along with my father. He's very self-centered. He has his own life. He never did anything with me. . . . He gives us a roof over our heads and pays for things. Now I owe him something. He's a dictator in the house. He acts that way with my mother too.

Bitterness against one of the parents, but some identification with the other.

I think that teenagers should be allowed to have responsibility, but, on the other hand, there are some who get more responsibility than they can handle. I had a girlfriend who had to take care of the whole household and never had any fun. When she said something, her parents said, "A little work don't hurt you." But the important thing is that parents should talk with their kids and should listen to them. It isn't enough to just provide for a child.

I know that adults think that teenagers are all wrong. I like adults who understand and listen. Too many are like my grandmother: if you tell her something, she gives you a lecture.

Both girls express the cry of all adolescents to be listened to, to be heard.

And here follow two of them who give us an even more intensive insight into their normal adolescent feelings of rebellion and their wish to be understood coupled with a rather calm and mature look at the adult world. The first one:

I do not think that all adults don't understand. My parents are young and my mother always understood me because she was close enough to my generation.

After my mother died when I was about thirteen years old, I had to live with my grandmother. She's not bad, but she does not understand. She likes to be old-fashioned. I mean by this, these people talk too much about *their* childhood. They tell us how they did not use the telephone or the car all the time, how they walked wherever they had to go. They don't realize that now towns are much bigger and that telephone and cars are a necessity. People don't live any more always across the street.

They talk about our dancing being immodest, like the Twist, but what about the Charleston? It probably was just as immodest in their time. They should take that into consideration.

I think adults should think more about the problems of the early age of dating. It gets younger and younger. Parents shouldn't allow this. Soon they will start dating when they are five years old. I think it can only be prevented by parents participating more in school activities and knowing about the friendships of their children. I know when there were school activities very few parents went to the schools, and every parent should know and keep up with the way school is taught today. I know, for instance, that my younger sister is already taught mathematics differently than I was taught. They should be informed on these subjects. Then they should not be so alien to their children and they should also discuss dating. They could help their child more to be an individual than to do only what the crowd does. It is important to keep that close to the younger one.

For instance, my little sister wrote to me that she needed me badly because I am more like a mother to her. She cannot talk to my grandmother because she is too old and the sisters that are younger than she are too young. She feels that I can understand her.

This girl criticizes adults, but she begins to see herself as one of them. She even thinks like an adult in relation to her younger sister and recognizes what should be done. The next girl pleads even more for some understanding, but she does not turn totally against the older generation:

I think what adults really don't understand is how we feel about things—like in a situation like this, like being pregnant. They say, "Well, why didn't you think about what would happen?" Well, I don't know. I guess you just don't think. I wish they could just read our minds and understand.

I don't think they understand our love relationships because it seems that in their day things like this didn't happen so often. I think you can blame it on the changing world. There have always been some unmarried mothers and I think they used to be shunned more than they are now. I am not saying it's all right, but now it happens so often in every community and people are willing to say, "You just made a mistake."

I probably don't feel any different from an adult, but I certainly would never do anything again, but it's hard. You love a guy an awful lot. If I have no feelings at all, the guy won't get to first base, and you have to love him a lot before you let him think you do.

These particular youngsters want the adult to help them with understanding themselves, to feel with their needs, wishes, difficulties, to help them develop standards and the strength to stay with them. They expect adults to make an effort to understand this new world with its changing values. To these girls the adult is a *person,* not a horribly brutal or anonymous power. When they fight or resent the adults, there is still tenderness, a wish to bridge the gap between themselves and their parents or parent substitutes. Most of these adolescent girls had some special difficulties with their mothers because of the complicated identification problem discussed earlier, but they could work them through successfully when a special effort was made or when a traumatic event (in these cases the pregnancy of the girl) hit the family. In most of these families the father was present and—even in spite of disappointment and conflicts—the girls felt a certain protection. The mothers were not in sharp rivalry with the teenagers.

The delinquent girl frequently comes from quite a different family background.

Families, especially parents, have been harshly blamed for juvenile delinquency. We have even gone so far—in some parts of this country—as to jail parents for the deeds committed by their children. This practice and mode of thinking were produced partially by the rightful understanding that children are not totally responsible for their acts. It was understood that there is a reason for behavior, that much of the dynamics of behavior have their roots in the family because it is the closest human association in our society. Yet to make the parent totally responsible means overlooking: (1) the pressures lying on the parents, too—the economic and social circumstances under which they act; (2) the many other human and environmental influences on the child; and (3) the child himself or herself.

Surely parents, family relationships, have a major impact on the girl's view of the world. Yet parents must not be made scapegoats. Most of the delinquent girls come from economically deprived families where the parents themselves live with frustration, where poverty not only means not having money, but also means ignorance, fear, and degradation. Children are no joy to these harassed parents; they are a nuisance, especially when they get older and assert themselves. They are the only handy objects on whom anger can be vented, because they are even more powerless than the parents who painfully hate their own impotence.

Many of the girls grew up in homes where no father was present, where mother had to be everything—and frequently could be noth-

ing because she too had no one to rely on. These girls have no experience with a father-person. Men hardly exist, or they exist as
occasional intruders in the family. The road to a healthy development toward womanhood through affection for the male and identification with mother simply does not exist.

A 16-year-old said:

> I ran away from home. I was tired of Dad. He hits me all the
> time. Mother hits me. They don't like me. We have seven kids.
> Where am I? I don't really know; I guess I'm kind of in the middle.
> Some of us always get treated badly especially when Mom and
> Dad drink. They always come after me. Since I ran away and said
> I wanted to stay with my aunt, they bring this up every time. They
> always bring up what once had happened. My God, they hit hard
> with a rope.

Here is physical abuse, here is the feeling of always being considered bad, of not belonging anywhere: "Where am I?" She might
have said: "Who am I?"

> I don't get along with my mother. My mother babies the younger
> ones, and doesn't care for older ones.

Here we see the special problem of the girl whose mother has not
become an adult. The baby was all right—it is a toy—the adolescent
girl especially becomes a rival. And just when the girl is in a situation where she can work through father-child relationships, the
adults may make it difficult for her without either giving her support or understanding her concern:

> Most people can't understand us. In fact, I can't understand
> myself. Now, when my mother and dad got married, I didn't want
> to call him "Dad" because my other dad was still alive. So, we had
> fights about everything. . . .
> So many things have happened to me since you saw me last.
> I have run away many times and have been returned many times.
> I *do* want to change, I really mean it, but I simply don't know how.
> I run away all the time because I need to get out.
> My goal is still to have a decent life—to get married, to have a
> nice family—but I simply don't know how to get to that. It's excit-
> ing to get into trouble. I like to go out to drink, to be in parties.
> I don't know really why I am that way. It started so very early.
> As I told you before, my parents were separated when I was
> ten years old, and my father was an alcoholic. I took the respon-

sibility for all the kids. I did all the cooking. Perhaps it was too much for me. I don't know. I surely rebelled and ran off every night.

The ten-year-old tried to be mother. But when puberty with its yearning, its thirst, and its confusion came, the role could not be continued. Since nobody shouldered part of her burden, the total load was thrown off. Over and over again the girls talk of harsh and confusing behavior.

> My father gave me such a beating when I was little that I was black and blue from the beating. All the time he was an alcoholic and he beats us all the time. My mother married when she was fifteen years old. There are fourteen children.

> My mother married and divorced several times. My mother beat me terribly. My mother did awful things when she was drunk. Once she got mad at me and she pulled my arm completely out of its socket and broke it. I passed out and I screamed in pain for a long time. She choked me. I will never forget some of the awful things. . . .
> At times I get so frightened. How can I drink when I hated my mother for drinking so much?

> I want a foster home. My father doesn't give me the right supervision. I want discipline. I don't say this just to please people. I don't mean punishment. I mean somebody who cares. . . .

> When my Dad isn't drunk I can be proud of him. . . . But all my life I can only remember drinking and fighting.

> I have a terrible father. I hate him. He was so strict. He was always beating us. He drank a lot. He sure is no good example. Maybe he wants me to be different from what he is and what he does but he sure does it terribly. Mother is okay but she doesn't do anything.

> My dad is strange. When I brought home some fine nice boys he seemed not to like them. He said they were drips. It seems to me that he liked hoodlums better.

The confusion, terror, and feeling of abandonment are even more increased by a hazard girls are exposed to: incestuous relationships with fathers are more frequent than is usually assumed. The adolescent girl is exceedingly frightened by this and often does not dare tell anyone about it. Guilt, especially toward the mother, is enormous. Some girls were forced through brutality into these relationships, some through various forms of persuasion. The latter ones felt especially guilty because they knew that they had responded positively. The experience filled all of them with almost nameless terror, so that they tried to repress it. If the situation was not known to the court, girls rarely mentioned it, even to the researcher. Yet in group discussions with other teenagers or in talks with a girlfriend, they had to relieve themselves.

Here is a sixteen-year-old talking:

> He wouldn't even let me go to the show by myself. I had to go with him or I couldn't go at all.
>
> But you know what happened to him, Sue? He was at that federal prison for seven years with all those men and I used to come to see him. I was growing up, you see. And I was beginning to look like a woman, and I used to come in there and sit on his lap. He's got a warped mind. He sat in there too long and I guess he started to think of me as his woman and not his daughter.
>
> He came out and it was just terrible. It was just like I was his wife. But you know how dumb I am. I couldn't think anything like that of him. When he did things like that, I used to think that he was just being strict because he didn't want me to go out and get pregnant or anything like that. But it wasn't true. I was just blind. He wanted me to be *his;* not his daughter. My own father!

There is little recourse for a girl in such a situation because of the harsh punitive attitude in our communities.

A fourteen-year-old had become so frightened of the advances her father made, that she finally told her mother only to be beaten up by both parents for telling such "lies." When things became unbearable she went to the police. It was proven she had told the truth. The father was sent to the penitentiary. Since the names and offenses of adults may be published in the newspapers, his name and his offense were published in the local paper. This was a small community and, therefore, the girl's situation immediately became public. She was treated like an outcast by everyone. She was sent to a delinquency institution because no other resources were available. This little fourteen-year-old was begging visitors to take her with them, just to some home! Fear and guilt were so overwhelming that she woke up screaming during the night. Listen:

> I started to think about death. I never want to die, never! And I think of my parents. If something happens to them while I'm here, I *will* die. I can't stand to think of Dad dying in a prison.
>
> I dream nights about Dad. He always chases me terribly. It is a nightmare! I dream he was so mean to me! I dream about mother in a car accident. It scares me. I sit in class in school, and I see Dad

passing by. I am so scared what he will do to me. He could break out of prison. I'm scared to death!

Guilt, fear, shame, and the eternal wish to be a child, to be wanted.

Emotions about mothers are strong and highly ambivalent. The reason for this is rebellion but also an unconscious need to respect mother so that one can keep one's self-respect. Girls looked for reasons why mothers acted the way they did, and they showed an unusual amount of drive to help their mothers. They did not always put it into action, but it was as if they had become the adult and mother was dependent on them:

> My mother even used to use dope. She is my problem. I feel responsible for her. Why? She's my mother and I love her.

This fifteen-year-old girl had been removed early from her home because the children in the family were greatly neglected. The mother drank, was promiscuous, and seemed unable to take care of the children. Though the girl often declared that she did not want to end up like her mother and that she felt that mother had not been the kind she would have hoped for, she still felt close to her.

It is known that all children, especially those who are rejected at home, tend to cling to their parents. I got the impression that the adolescent girl has an increased need to hold on—especially to the mother, even while fighting her. This same girl expressed her need to protect her mother very intensely:

> I have so many problems I wouldn't know where to start. You see I was seven years old when I was taken away from my family. I was *taken* away. I was five years in a foster home, and then two years at home and then back two years in the foster home. They took me away from my mother. They just took me! I belong to the state. I didn't like the foster home. Nobody believes me. It is a terrible place. I got into lots of trouble. I ran away, I took things, I was with boys. The foster mother always threw it up to me. She always threw my past up to me. There wasn't a day that she wouldn't tell me what I have done. She turned me in this time, too. I never want to go back to her.
>
> I want to go home to my mother. She drinks. She constantly has headaches, but I am the only one who understands her. They don't understand her. My two brothers are in foster homes, and they don't mind. They don't belong to her anymore, but I do. I always will. I understand what she is up against. It is like this: my mother is a weak person. She is just weak. Her friends drag her down. I understand her weakness. *They* say, "She is just doing it to have fun."

She has no fun. She is just weak. When I am around she does not drink so much. I am good for her. I need to help her. . . .

When I am away from her it all builds up inside me. I can't stand it. When I was with my mother I never ran away. I went to school. The one who *is* my mother *is* my mother.

The girl often takes total guilt for her misbehavior upon her own shoulders. She resents it deeply if the mother is blamed by outsiders.

As long as my mother lives, I want to be near her. She is too lonesome. . . . It is my fault that she aged. I must make it up to her. She was a pretty young woman when I had my first baby and she got grey hair. I don't want to kill my mother. I'm guilty because I let her down.

I ran away three weeks ago to my mother, but there is no real home. My mother is worse at home. My father almost killed my mother because she acted so badly.

I think I understand what's the matter with her. I think she wants to travel and have adventure, but the children have kept her down and she can't do it.

The experiences that some of the youngsters had continue even when they are removed from their own homes. It is difficult to find good foster homes for such girls, because foster parents must tolerate very upsetting behavior. Often they give up or—in anger—continue the pattern the girls were used to. Fifteen-year-old Judy describes such an experience:

I was with this other foster mother for nine years, and she was bitching at me too, telling me not to do this, do that. She used to make us learn our alphabet, and I didn't learn mine until I was in the sixth grade, because I just couldn't learn it, and I couldn't pronounce words.

One day I couldn't pronounce this word "gits," and I still can't pronounce it. I say "gits" and it's "gets," like I "git" something. And so she whipped me that whole day. She wouldn't let me go to school. Her house . . . , you know, you can go from the kitchen to the dining room, from the dining room to the living room and living room to the hall and back into the kitchen, and you know, just go around. So I was running around, and she was whipping me. And every night we used to come and she'd whip us, me and this other boy who stayed there. We couldn't learn our alphabets, so . . .

She used to mix her food, you know, the left-overs. She would put it all together and cook it, and it tasted just terrible. So, once I didn't want to eat it, so I vomited and—maybe I shouldn't say this—and I vomited it, and she made me eat it all. She made me eat every last bit of it. And so I was getting the last spoon in my mouth, and I heaved it up again, and I started eating it again, but she said I did not have to eat it. And the rest of the kids had to sit there and watch me do it.

Are your sensibilities hurt, reader? Do you feel nauseated by this small glimpse into the cruelty of humanity? Then I must remind you that this is not an invention of a sick mind, that many of the girls I saw have lived through such unspeakable experiences.

My dad is in the penitentiary. He forced me. Oh, it made no difference to me. My dad married four times. I keep dreaming of my dad. I dream that he kills me, and I dream also of the other man who forced me into sex relations. My brother held a knife against my throat while they did it.

Listen to her "it made no difference to me" followed by the nightmares. On the outside she appears hard, unfeeling. This is what she must be to protect herself from falling apart.[7]

Ida's mother ironed the girl's dress with a hot iron while she had it on her body, burning her severely in order to teach her not to muss it. There are many more subtle cruelties: being degraded, being pushed around like a thing, not a person. Many of the girls blamed themselves or threw the hate on others, not on their own parents. Most frequently they complained that nobody was willing to listen to them. A fourteen-year-old, bitter and sophisticated beyond her years, summarized it by saying:

What I especially don't like about adults and especially teachers is that they don't let you finish what you want to say. When you start to explain something, they say, "Oh no! oh no . . . !" I was before the judge. I don't know what to say about him. *He is just another one who has just a bunch of answers.* I wasn't scared. Nothing scares me anymore. I just have to face the facts. Why do I have to do that? I tell you, I have always been afraid of everything. I was even afraid to face the class. I learned that you just have to know that this is life and you have to face it.

What this girl means by "facing life" is a hard-bitten, distrustful cynicism directed toward all adults. She closes them out. You "take" them, but they mean nothing. They do not care about her. They

[7] See Gisela Konopka and Jack V. Wallinga, "Stress as a Social Problem," *The American Journal of Orthopsychiatry*, XXXIV: 3 (April 1964), 536-42.

do not listen. They have just a "bunch of answers" unrelated to *her* real questions. This is the way she feels and to which she reacts.

Have we ever completely, and in its last consequence, faced the fact that most delinquent youngsters meet adults *only* in the form of authority without the component of loving care which good parents add to it? Authority to them is never combined with the occasional indulgence of grandparents or aunts or family friends. To the child in a happy family the angry father is also a good father; mother is limit-setting *and* giving. Thus authority can be accepted. But many of the girls miss this and the authority they meet outside the family is made even more formidable and frightening because few, if any, of these adults belong to the world of the teenager. Most of the teachers, social workers, judges, church representatives, policemen, do not live in their neighborhood, do not experience the noise, the smell, the fighting, the deprivation, the confusion, in which most of the girls grow up. They are strangers with power. The group workers who once could walk through the toughest district without any fear because they actually were "neighbors" have become rare. A Jane Addams could be accepted as an authority because she lived in the slums, delivered the baby in an emergency when somebody knocked at her door in the night to call for help. She took into her house the prostitute when the girl's lover beat her up. She knew them and they knew her—so her voice could be heard. The gym teacher who lived around the corner and went on trips with the neighborhood kids, the painter who sat in front of his house and gave the children some paper and color to smear with while he worked, have become practically non-existent. Among professionals today, perhaps the only ones who still have this kind of relationship are the youth-gang workers. Yet they are few, and they rarely work with girls. The same applies to neighborhood clergymen. There are not many in the deprived city areas, and those who work there focus their attention on boys. To the girl, therefore, most people in authority are not really "people." They cannot feel any common ground with them. Their meeting with authority is symbolized by the DESK. What an alien thing this desk is to deprived children! It is a piece of furniture that does not exist in their homes. They have never seen somebody working calmly at one. They meet this thing only as a kind of barrier between themselves and someone who has power over them: the teacher, the social worker, the psychologist, the judge. They have never known a friendly consultation with a doctor at a desk. They may have met physicians in a hospital or a clinic but rarely as confidants or as equals to their parents, the way a middle-class child experiences them. Across this formidable barrier the adult metes out judgment or gives instruction or makes the almost impossible demand of trust!

In my research, sitting side by side in interviews, talking while drying the dishes, and especially engaging in group discussions eliminated this symbolic barrier and made communication easier. The alienation from the adult world was immense, though. To the girls "they"—the grownups—were not real; they were massive walls, but no faces. They were not really human.

I don't understand adults. The adults say they never got into trouble, that they never had any problems. How is that possible? I don't believe them. They lie. . . . Why do they act so perfect? I think they just try to push us into the ground and make us feel like nothing.

Sure I go to the social worker and I tell how much it helps me, but really it hasn't helped me any. It's just the way, you know. . . . If I say it has helped me, and make them think it has helped me . . . , it's just a way of getting out.

I can't talk at all to my social worker even though I try.

The social worker gave me only disappointments. She never explained to me, for instance, why I didn't get out. She only said she didn't know me well enough. Why didn't she try?

They keep us here at the training school for too long. You know how it feels when you get in? You just can't believe that it is you that is here. It's a shock! But people don't understand. You put up a front but you are just shocked. I wanted to go home after awhile for Christmas but they didn't let me. I asked the social worker, and the social worker never told me the reason for it. I ran away three times, but I couldn't find my mother so I got back. I can't stand foster homes. I ran away.

I can't talk with anybody. I can't talk with the social worker. What makes me most mad is when she says, "I understand." How can she understand? She doesn't understand at all! I want to be free! I can't be locked in in the evenings! I wish she could understand, but she doesn't understand. I was supposed to go on parole in December, but I ran in November. I was supposed to go out in June, and I ran in May. Do you understand that? She says that I don't want to be home, but that isn't true, and I know that.

I like the way I am. Those young social workers can't understand anything. They have never lived. I don't want to say it, but I have to tell them so. I think I can make it the way I am. . . .

And these people, they say things to you. "You come to me with all your problems, and I'll help you." And then they turn around and tell everybody else in here and discuss you with other people, and they will tell you one thing and mean another. I think we should sit in on our own staff meetings so we have a voice to say about ourselves too.

The greatest problem is that nobody understands. . . . They don't understand. . . . They only know what's in the books. They don't know life. What I did just isn't in the books! I stayed out at night, stole cars, robbed stores, and we were a whole gang. The boy I went with isn't a bad boy. People don't understand that either.

I think we just get into an age where many of us get into trouble. Most of us just have nobody to sit down with and just talk, and it seems that we can never talk with our parents. It used to be very hard for me to talk to any people. It is now a little better, but now I perhaps could talk to people like you where I know it don't get into the record.

One can hear the hostility and the hopelessness. The social workers, like the girls' mothers, frequently receive the brunt of the distrust and anger. Others, like the director of the institution or judges and even teachers, are so removed that they are only "they," no one the girls can recognize as part of their world. They do not even speak the same language.

I want to be a missionary and a veterinarian. I love animals. But think of those stupid people on the Commission—they talk to you with stupid questions that keep you here.

Now, that guy asked me what I wanted to be, and when I told him I wanted to be a veterinarian, he asked me questions, and I didn't know all the answers. For instance: What does a missionary do first? I told him that I thought a missionary helps people to understand God. But no, that's not what he meant. How do I know what he meant? Well, he tells me that a missionary starts first to learn the language of the people and tries to get the people to like him. Okay, but why does he expect me to know all that?

And because these adults and the girls cannot understand each other, authority is frequently seen as the force which prevents even positive attempts:

Now I want to do something on my own. I don't want "mending." My boyfriend gave me something whole, something that made me a whole person. When I had found a job I made fifty-two cents an hour. I paid my rent, I paid my food, and I sent some money to my sister. My probation officer destroyed that, but I will try again.

The probation officer may have been totally justified in what she did, but communication is hard to establish when trust has not grown. Yet the *wish* to find adults who understand is surprisingly strong. The girls are cautious and wary, yet so very much in need of people who are supportive. See the struggle of a nineteen-year-old who begins to believe that perhaps not all adults are bad, but who has to fight the distrust of her whole peer group as well as her own:

> Do I find strength in anything else? If you mean religion, no. I do not feel strong enough for it. And I have not found any great meaning in life. I begin to see that life is different than I thought it was. For instance, here among the inmates you are not supposed to like any officer. They are supposed to be your enemies. I can't always feel that way. I think they could help. But, on the other hand, they too, must prove to me that they don't just talk, but do the right things. For instance, one of them recently came into the room here, and one of the girls was very upset about something, and this girl snapped at the officer. So this officer said, "If you are mad at someone else, you don't have to snap at me." Well, a little time later, I went into her office, and she snapped at me. She had done the same thing that she had just told the girl not to do.

If the adult allows himself to be a person, to come closer, the still existing capacity to trust is surprising, the need almost overwhelming.

> There is one adult in my whole life whom I trust and to whom I look up to: he is a policeman from the Morals Squad. You should meet him. . . . I can talk to him frankly. He is a man who knows what he is talking about, and he is always open with me.
>
> He knew me as a child. He was different from all the other people—the social worker or anyone—I have ever met. He is interested in *me*. He tells me what I do wrong, but he *cares*. That is the main thing.

The girls especially resent what they term the "phoniness" of adults. By this they mean their insincerity, their not living up to or practicing the ideals which they present and preach to the girls. Again, because the authority figure is so removed and unreal, because he confronts the girl only with demands and restrictions—never appearing as a play companion or a giving person—the girl retaliates by expecting perfection. *All* adolescents look for more excellence in the adult world than it can give. *All* adolescents feel disappointed when they discover the "feet of clay." This disappointment is mixed with a certain satisfaction because adult imperfection gives the youngsters some justification for their own shortcomings, which they feel so acutely. It also justifies their rebellion. This is intensified in the girl who has never experienced a warm human relationship with an adult. When this adolescent girl realizes that adults do not live up to their own precepts, her feelings for them turn to contempt and, so far as she is concerned, completely justify her discounting them.

> I consider myself really an adult, no longer a teenager. But I still rebel against authority. They are so stupid. The way I figure it, everybody in this world who don't do exactly what he should do tries to put the blame on someone else. So the adults blame the teenagers because they themselves are not so good. It bothered me an awful lot. It bothers me a little less now. Since ever that I can think, I kept out of their way. As a small child I kept out of trouble by just keeping out of their way.

The intense emotions about adult hypocrisy reach to the core of the girl's being, her conflicts in the sexual area. Delinquent boys also talk about the "phony" adults as they too reject them. Their disagreements and objections seem to be on a less deeply imbedded layer of their emotions. They point to contradictions in relation to business ethics and what they are told to do. (Tax evasion was at a certain period a favorite justification for all kinds of misbehavior in boys.) They hate forgotten or easily made and broken promises.

The girls struggle with the "double standard" and are often in a situation where either those "phony" adults can exploit the girl or she can exploit them. This creates deep wounds. The girl either deadens the pain by increased acting out or "freezes" the wound by denial of any feeling. "It's the good citizen who seeks us out for prostitution," or "My mother does exactly what she tells me not to do" are typical responses to demands of change made of the girls who have become promiscuous.

Yet just because the hurt is so deep, there is a readiness to accept adults, a cry for their help, a wish to open up. If adults could just see them as the children they are in addition to the frightened and experienced women they seem to be, if they only could meet them as people, not as little criminals with a terrible past! If only the adults themselves would get *faces,* not just blank masks on top of judgment gowns!

The little fourteen-year-old who was tortured by the nightmares of a vengeful father sobbed,

> I had to talk to the minister. I insisted that they call him one night. I told him I was getting so confused. Things seem right but they seem wrong. I even kicked out my screen because I couldn't stand anything. I got involved in school. . . . I don't want to talk about the past all the time. I want to talk about the future.

The vivacious fifteen-year-old whose beauty and brilliant mind strike one like sunshine, but who has behind her a history of purse snatching, car stealing, and truancy, hides behind this sunny exterior a desperate lack of self-confidence. She can express what many of them look for:

> I wish more people who have gone through what we have would admit it when they are older, instead of always pretending that they were perfect. It would help.

And a little later:

> If we could just do something here that is of benefit to other people. I like art and architecture, and we should learn more about that. You know, girls also like to build things, not only boys. But the main thing we need inside or outside is people who respect us and who can gain the respect of the girls. Somebody like Miss Smith, the teacher. She can really gain the respect of all the girls. We like her, and we respect her. She can laugh with us, and she can also make demands on us. If she says something, she means it.

What they need is a person who respects them and whom they can respect, a person who can laugh with them but who does not laugh at them. Behind the hatred and misunderstanding lies much of their own incapacity to understand themselves and their feeling of helplessness.

The Impact of Prejudice

Loneliness is increased with disastrous results of individual suffering and harm to the whole fabric of society by the terrible illness of our human community: prejudice, and especially prejudice based on race. It hits most sharply in adolescence, just at a period in the child's development when the need for acceptance is greatest, when the feeling of self-worth is precarious and needs much support. It also hits hardest at that age because, even in integrated communities, the cruelly subtle social segregation begins. It is even fostered by many who intellectually have accepted that "all men are equal," but whose emotions are still haunted by some irrational fear of the "assault by the dark."

This fear of some unnamed sex attack is often provoked in race relations, and the girls were deeply concerned with it. They resented the implications and the general feeling of superiority of one race over another.

Some girls experienced rejection only because of economic or class distinctions, but this was less frequent. A sixteen-year-old spoke for several of these when she said that her trouble started when the family moved from a working-class environment to the suburbs:

> The kids were uppity. I couldn't compete with the way they dressed. I just was alone.

And an older girl, a Negro girl who grew up in a predominantly white school, recalled:

> I had no trouble at home. I have lovely parents. . . . I grew up in the city [a working-class district] and then we moved to the suburbs. Kids were so different. I couldn't find any close friends. That is about the time when the trouble started.

> Everything was all right when I was little but when I became a teenager I had practically no friends. And I wanted a friend so badly!

A sixteen-year-old Negro youngster—beautiful, alive, sparkling —with a history of stealing and prostitution told me:

> I lived in the suburbs with a distant relative. I never had many friends. The kids in the neighborhood were too young.
> I had no school friends. Well, I was the only Negro girl in school. The others never invited me to their homes. When I became twelve years old, I felt the boys were embarrassed with me so I couldn't have any friends.
> My first true friend was another girl of my age who moved next

door. She was not snooty. Well, she did a lot of swearing and stealing. But she took me out to meet the boys and we played records. . . .

The separation from those to whom this youngster originally thought she belonged—and to whom she should belong according to the basic ethos of our society—drove her into companionship with another "undesirable," and the long road of delinquency was started.

To some, being "shunned" becomes so overwhelming that other relationships offered are not enough—or perhaps they are not offered skillfully and intensely enough. Sixteen-year-old, slim, dark-skinned Vera had become quiet, docile. She retreated, she sucked her thumb, and she remembered:

> When I didn't go to school I would just hang around with the kids. We didn't do anything special. I just didn't want to go to school. I was so lonely. I was the only Negro girl in my school. The kids aren't always nice. The older boys made dirty remarks when I passed by.
>
> I was in a group at the Community Center, and I went to the NAACP picnic. I liked that, but I couldn't talk with people about my troubles.
>
> Maybe they would like me to talk about them, but I can't.

Vera's way out of all this unhappiness is quite common among those who do not feel wanted. They really have given up; sometimes, in fact, they have taken over the attitudes of those who despise them. They are delinquent usually in a "passive" form: they truant, they do not answer questions, they fail, they hang around. They are often the youngsters who infuriate adults because they seem so remote and unapproachable.

American Indian girls seem to confirm the belief that "Indians don't speak." But they really hold back only because otherwise they would cry too loudly. One American Indian girl spoke of the hurt of hypocrisy and said,

> I know many Indians who are actually very smart, but you see, we are afraid to show it. We are afraid of being judged ridiculous. We are afraid they will say, "Oh, it's only a dumb dirty Indian." So many give up and don't make good grades.

She and the others she talked about had decided that there was no use in combatting the prejudice they had been exposed to. It was easier to act the way it was expected of them. This girl was solemn, usually uncommunicative, and she failed in school. Yet, when she allowed herself to take off the mask of incompetence, she proved to be a highly capable person.

Seventeen-year-old Norma had been shuttled between reservation and city, back and forth. She felt like a stone pushed back and forth on a checkerboard with nothing to say about herself, and nothing to look forward to:

> Yes, people are prejudiced about Indians. Many girls and also some of the staff. And I am a half-breed. I dislike myself.

Doris, fourteen, a member of my young group of probationers, also belonged in this group of youngsters who have given up. Her home was overcrowded, unhappy, deprived. Her Indian heritage was considered inferior, even by her family. Doris could have been beautiful, with her large dark eyes and her black hair, but her beauty was hidden by rolls of fat and general neglect. Doris hardly spoke at first, and when she spoke it was only in a whisper. Yet what she said should be heard like thunder:

> I am in a lot of trouble at school. The teachers don't understand. I am getting suspended for talking in class and because I laugh. They don't do it with any other kids. They pick on me. They don't like me. They always get mad at me—almost all the teachers.
> I don't like school. It's too early in the morning. It's so cold when you get up, and I don't understand what they are teaching. One of the teachers said she would help me if I come after school. I have never gone. I am afraid.

How can a girl like Doris know what it means to be quiet? Who knows why she laughs? I learned in the group that laughter was Doris's way of crying. Who in our modern age remembers the horror of getting up when the room is ice cold—especially when there is no one who really cares whether you do or don't? And if help is offered, Doris cannot accept it. She is afraid.

The teacher knows only that this stubborn youngster does not appear even though she offered help. The youngster thinks, "They don't like me." The gulf between them is wide. The girl herself loses more and more the hope of becoming anything. She continues:

> People tease me because I am an Indian. They are mean. When I get mad, they say, "She is on the warpath." One girl called me a "black Indian." I knocked her out.

Everybody says I might be pretty if I would lose some weight. But I am afraid to lose weight because then I might be having too many boyfriends. I am afraid of that. I like boys, but I don't want to have too many boyfriends.

I would like to live on another planet and see how it is there. If I can't, I would like to live in another country. I would like to see many things as one sees on TV. I want to be rich. I want to have lots of nice things—cars and horses—and I would like to be able to have a ranch. I want to get it by inheriting a lot of money, not work for it. Well, if that isn't possible, I would like to go to a fashion school and study fashion design. I want to get married later and have just one little girl like my youngest sister. I would also like to see one real football game, not just on TV.

We see the dreamlike quality of her wishes to escape the reality of cold, disorganization, prejudice, and poverty. (*"I would like to see one real football game, not just on TV."*) We see her feeling of being singled out as unwanted. How can she otherwise understand her situation? We see her fear of trying to improve, even to the point of not wanting to lose weight because then she might have to cope with the problem of being liked by boys—something she wants and yet fears. Home, school, and neighborhood offer nothing that gives her the feeling of being an important human being. So Doris dreams, truants, does "nothing," and goes from detention to institution and back to her home to start the endless cycle again.

Yet others, singly and usually with deep anger, fight the position into which they are put. If there is some understanding and support from adults, the anger may not turn to hate. Contrast the account of a fifteen-year-old Indian girl who had some support with the account of a Negro girl of the same age who met constant rejection. The latter is the same girl who had been forced by her foster mother to eat what she had thrown up. First the Indian youngster:

I have been to a white school and I learned a lot. I can mix with anyone without being afraid, and I am proud to be an Indian. White children are often prejudiced. I remember one of them who said that the others shouldn't mix with us, because we were dirty Indians and had lice. I was furious. And I told him that if I had lice I would just give them to him!

The principal of that school was good though. He called an assembly and told the kids they should be proud to have Indian children with them because we were the first inhabitants on this continent.

Now the other one:

> You said I should just say what I want to tell the world. I'll shoot. The worst is prejudice. I live in what they call the "colored belt." Boy, have we had it! The teachers in school say "nigger," and that is true! But I will not take that! I will fight.
>
> Boy, one teacher in school once asked me, "What is the color of pygmies in Africa?" What does he think I am? Why should he ask *me* when I was the only Negro in that class? Why should I know everything about Africans? So when he asked me that, I said, "Look at your own grandmother." That made him mad, and he threw me out.
>
> When they had that problem about desegregation in the South, one teacher brought to class a picture of a Negro hanging in a noose, and it said that this would happen to anybody who fought segregation. . . .
>
> Some Negroes think they are too fine for us, especially those from the Urban League. I guess I am prejudiced, too. I hate white people. One Negro woman I talked to belongs to the Black Muslims. She says that God created the black people first and then they watered it down and then some people became brown and then they watered it down again until some people became white. If they watered it down some more there would be nothing. So the white people are close to nothing. They *are* nothing. Then, when I tell that to the girls, they say I am prejudiced, and I want to fight prejudice. I guess they are right. I like some individuals, but I just don't like the white race.

She had to retaliate to keep herself intact. Her state of mind lent itself easily to personal abuse or exploitation by fanatics.

To all the girls I met, the fight for racial justice and against discrimination was a *personal* one, regardless of whether they themselves belonged to the majority or a minority group. It was not a cause for which they fought by joining organizations or movements. In general, they had little knowledge or understanding of civic responsibility and democratic process. Government was outside their reach; it was not "we," only "it"—something one could not trust. It was again a faceless, anonymous power, over which they themselves could not imagine having any influence. It was part of the "phony," unjust world around them. Aware of the fact that American democracy demands acceptance of all people as equal, they see the contradictory practices and attitudes as another proof of a hostile and unreliable world. If prejudice was expressed by someone in authority outside the family, adolescent rebellion was stronger than the expression of deep hurt. When it came from someone in the family there was ambivalence, sometimes a wish to convince them and—if this did not work—deep sadness. When it came from the outside, it made the girl feel justified in her general distrust:

> I have only belonged to a club when I was in the Indian orphanage. We were happy there. We said, "Don't associate with white people." I guess I was prejudiced. I still am a bit. I am a little bit better now, but I liked the orphanage because everybody was the same.
>
> Here there is race prejudice. The teacher is prejudiced. For instance, they always treat girls very different who are Negro or Indian. I got up one day in class and I asked the teacher whether I could ask a question. I asked if he would treat girls in public schools on the outside the same way he treats us. And he said he had to treat us different, because we were different. But we are no different from other people. I said that to him, and all he said was "Shut up." I spoke up because it makes me so mad.

The most angry comments came when the area of sex relations was touched. Over and over the girls expressed their resentment that people were supposed to be looked at as "people" but that (so they felt) everyone was especially negative toward them when they "mixed," which meant interracial dating. This was the case not only with dating between white and Negro, but also when there was dating between other racial or ethnic groups. A nineteen-year-old Indian girl said,

> My boyfriend is a Negro. My counsellor is very prejudiced. I know because she freezes up when I want to talk about it. My mother is not prejudiced. Colored people took care of us when we were little. They were our neighbors. I was scared of them when I was a baby. I sometimes even ran away. I am no longer afraid, and my fiancé is one of the gentlest people I know.

An older Caucasian girl:

> People don't understand young people. My folks especially don't understand my love. . . . He is a Mexican. . . . They always are against someone from another race.
>
> He changed my whole life. He made me feel at home. His family makes me feel good. My mother disowned me because I suggested an interracial marriage.

And another:

My little boy is part Negro. My family is dead set against Negroes. I have a half-sister who is half Indian. I asked her whether she would welcome me and my baby. She said, "My three little girls are white and I can't expose them to that." I will have a lot to live down, but I will do anything for my baby.

My mother said, "If you go out with a nigger, I am not your mother." I only said, "Were you ever?"

I did like my father. But when I was home I argued with him. I asked my father why he called everybody a "nigger."

Many of the girls themselves are not sure of their own attitudes. They do not allow themselves to work through their conflicts. If the adult shows prejudice, then resistance stiffens and they hit out angrily. It was mostly in group discussions that the girls used the opportunity to speak up frankly and admit ambivalence, even prejudice. They felt safer when other girls were present. The older adolescent girls in a closed institution tackled this problem at the first session. I quote from the summarized account:

Without transition the discussion became very violent and turned to the subject of "going with" Negroes. They referred to something that they had discussed among themselves the evening before, where they apparently had been in sharp conflict with each other.

Rita said that she has found out that Negroes aren't worth anything. She, too, has gone with Negroes. All this talk about discrimination was nonsense. Every other minority group has been able to overcome discrimination. Why not Negroes? They just feel sorry for themselves.

Bertha protested vehemently, saying that people were prejudiced and that Negroes were kept down.

Rita again insisted that the Negroes who went with them were doing this only to lower the girls and to make them feel inferior.

Bertha took this very personally and shouted that her child was a good child even if the child was half Negro. She insisted that her life had only taken on meaning since the child had arrived.

Rose said that was all right. It was nonsense that they were talking so much about going with white or Negro men. Why didn't they play it safe and go only with women?

During the discussion, Peggy tried several times to bring the discussion toward her own problem, but the others were obviously not interested. They continued with their subject.

After some time, when the argument became again very heated, the group worker suggested that perhaps it might be helpful if she would summarize where they stood. Obviously they did agree on the fact that one could not judge a person according to his color; that a person was a person; that some Negroes were fine people, and some were not, just the same as this was the case with white people. The problem they were discussing was a question regarding the character of people with whom they were going. An agreement was not reached, but the summary calmed down Bertha, who had shouted that she would not participate in any more discussions where so much prejudice was expressed.

Rose stated calmly that it was high time for them to learn to talk about things without always shouting at each other.

This open sharing of feelings of which they were ashamed and this beginning of real discussion—not just shouting at each other— were new and very important experiences which helped them work their way through confused adolescent emotions intensified by an even more confusing and contradictory world.

4. THE IMPACT OF CULTURAL CHANGE ON WOMEN'S POSITION

All right, Go ahead!
What's in a name?
I guess I'll be locked into
As much as I'm locked out of! [1]

One of the keys to understanding the girl in conflict is her feeling of loneliness in the faceless, anonymous world of adults.

The second major key is rapid cultural change and its particular impact on the adolescent girl. Culture and mores are always changing, but usually the change occurs slowly, imperceptibly. An accomplished change does not present many conflicts to individuals. It is the state of flux, with its accompanying contradictions of values and expectations, which places a special burden on the young and the old who are caught in it. Rapid technical development makes different demands, and modern society places emphasis on values which are quite different from those stressed in the old, agrarian

[1] Edna St. Vincent Millay, "The Prisoner," *A Few Figs from Thistles* (New York: Harper and Row, Publishers, Inc.). Copyright 1922, 1950 by Edna St. Vincent Millay. Reprinted by permission of Norma Millay Ellis.

society. Yet the most significant change taking place in the twentieth century is not technical advancement; it is the emancipation of women. It is true that modern technology—the rapid development of the airplane, for example—has made communication easier; that television has brought the world to the doorstep of people who previously had been locked away in a narrow environment. But these are all external changes.

The emancipation of women involves the whole fabric of family life. It is changing the basic family structure from a hierarchical institution with the father as the head of the household to a democratic "Gestalt" (entity) with more equalitarian roles for husband and wife. It is bringing about the acceptance of women as *persons,* not symbols, but persons with highly individual differences. This latter change is not yet total; it is in transition. The concept of "femininity," which seemed rather clear only a half century ago, is now vague. Is it "feminine" or not to aspire to be an astronaut or a physician? Are slacks not "feminine"? There will be different responses.

Much has been written about the conflict created in women by this change, and especially about the conflict in the intellectual and professional woman. I found that today's young college girl seems to have fewer problems with her role in society than did her older sister in the 1920s. Perhaps the change has already begun to become more stabilized in this generation. A nineteen-year-old said calmly,

> The question of work versus having a family is no problem to most of us. We don't see any contradiction. We will work just as hard as any man to get our degree and we will choose what we are capable of doing. We will have dates and we want enjoyment and love just like the boys, but I want to postpone marriage until we both have finished our education. I want to have children and I will stay at home with them while they are young. But I expect to continue my professional work at a certain time in my life; I don't know when, exactly.

Or another one:

> Labor-saving devices are fine. The washing machine is the liberation of women. I love to keep house, but it doesn't have to be drudgery. The labor-saving devices will help me to raise my children much better and to contribute to society.

The changing status of women has very different meaning to the girl from a lower income group. Very little recognition has been given to this fact. The middle-class woman assumes that her own fight for the right to work, for liberation from the notorious "three K's" (Küche, Kinder, Kirche—kitchen, children, church), is the fight of *all* women. Many programs—even recent ones, such as those concerned with helping the drop-out—are based on this same assumption. But this assumption does not hold for the working-class girl. The awareness of the almost reversed dynamics of woman's emancipation on working-class girls has startling consequences.

The major point is that "working women" are not the product of the emancipation movement at all, that occupations outside the home are nothing new to the laborer. All through the centuries, women have worked exceedingly hard, often in the most physically demanding jobs and in the least desirable jobs. They have been the field hands, the servants, the washerwomen, and, in the industrial era, the factory workers. They had to leave their families for paid work, which was always especially backbreaking. Laundry workers stood for hours, bent over tubs, lifting heavy sheets, using muscle power to wring out the clinging, wet, bulky garments. Women stood —and still stand in some parts of the world—for many hours in cold water, scrubbing, beating, and finally lifting the heavy baskets with wet clothes. On the roads in the Far East one still meets women walking along carrying huge loads to the markets while their male companions ride the donkey or the camel. Scrub women worked hard, bending, kneeling, dragging themselves across the floor, not only of their own homes but those of others and of large public buildings. (It is significant that cleaning tools which allowed for a more comfortable upright position came into use when men were employed in cleaning occupations.) Waitresses worked endless hours standing on their feet, carrying dishes, frequently being treated like inferior servants, not like employees. In industry—even today— women usually do physically heavy and very repetitive jobs. They rarely move up to become a foreman to oversee the work of others. In my own experience in the 1930s, I remember that it was customary for the women in factories to work at the work benches. They hammered metal, pushed around heavy baskets, or were at the drilling presses. Only men watched certain machines which needed intermittent care with little physical effort involved.

Women always worked, and worked hard. The opposition to women's role as a working partner actually decries only her entrance into the higher and more desirable positions. To those who have lived through the Nazi regime in Germany, this fact was brought home forcibly during its early months. Under the guise of bringing women back into the home, the regime's first attacks on women's employment were directed against the middle-class and especially against professional positions. Legislation was soon enacted to forbid a married woman to be employed as a teacher. No legislation and no propaganda were directed against women's work in manual labor, especially in household employment, though this was hard, poorly paid work and kept her for many long hours from her home.

The working girl, therefore, comes from a tradition of work outside the home—a tradition of exploitation. She could not consider work a privilege or a right to fight for. Her goal for centuries has been to get out of it as quickly as she could. Again, by tradition different from that for men, she had a way out: marriage, a good marriage. "Good" meant that she could find a husband who would take care of her financially, and of her children when they came.

Cultural mores demanded and demand that the man be gainfully employed always, whether he likes it or not. He must take care of himself and his family. This is the burden placed upon him. This inexorable demand made men get together to fight for better working conditions, for better pay. It is also the motive for many—the majority—to prepare themselves for such a life and to find means of advancement. Those who do not see such possibilities despair and give up. Their lack of opportunity is related to social and economic factors, but not to the fact that they are *men*.

In some respect, therefore, the "way out"—marriage—allows the woman a special privilege. It looks on the surface as if she is less "caught" than the man. Actually this has brought about poor job opportunities for working women. Women were—and still are— less motivated to improve their working conditions in general and their own position in particular. Society as a whole looks at typical women's occupations as inferior and temporary, and therefore offers less compensation. Very hard work is still not rewarded by good pay. Though thousands of women will have to make their living whether they stay single or are married, the dream of "being taken care of" prevents the individual girl from seeking an education, from preparing for some permanency in a working life. Her lack of opportunity is directly bound up with her being a woman. There is no tradition of a work ethos, no memory of the dignity of artisanship, in the history of women's labor. (Needlework presents an exception to this. There is a history of skill and pride in it, but it is not bound up with remuneration and the labor market.)

The constant, even well-meaning, appeal made by middle-class professional women to many of the delinquent girls to work hard and apply themselves, to see work as desirable, has completely disregarded this historical development. It is based on the different development of the fight for women's rights in the more intellectual woman who fought for the right to work while her far less privileged sister yearned to get away from having to work. To the working-class girl the attributes of life which accompany the possession of money are important, but it is difficult for her to accept the dreary hardship which goes with the kind of work she is condemned to. This is not just an individual shortcoming. It is the result of a long traditional neglect of women in the labor force.

The hopes and aspirations expressed by many of the delinquent girls show their view of marriage or a liaison as something that could take them away from the need to make a living. They know little of what marriage entails, and they often do not look forward to it. I simply is the "way out," unreal and romantic:

> What do I want to be? I would want to be an actress. I want everyone to be at my feet. They should all look up to me. I want lots of money and lots of clothes. Maybe I will marry a rich man who has all the money but maybe I won't marry at all. I don't really care for men.
>
> I want to finish high school and get married. If my husband is laid off then I'll have to go to work, but otherwise, I don't want to work. I like to keep a clean house. I've never thought about what I would do if I didn't keep house. I want to marry someone rich so that we have a pretty house and a swimming pool and can give the kids a lot of stuff. I want to have a nice car, nice clothes, nice furniture. I want to have a maid, but my husband shouldn't be lazy.

There is a fairy tale quality in what one fourteen-year-old has to say:

> I want to go to college and become a nurse, because my aunt is a nurse. School is okay, but I am not so good at it. . . . Well, when I get to be twenty-five, I want to be married, and have two kids, and live in a climate without snow—like California. I want a nice home—a yellow house. I might be a nurse part-time.
>
> My husband should have black wavy hair, brown eyes, and he should be tall. He should be a rich husband—like an office worker or a parole officer. He should be nice. What do I mean by "nice"? *Nice* means to be considerate to others. Some day I hope my children would go to college.

The more deprived the background, the stronger is the yearning to get out of the kind of life the girl knows. One fifteen-year-old

Indian girl is very descriptive and more realistic about what she wants, and her wishes include marriage and work:

> I want to be married and have children and work. I want to have three children. The oldest must be a boy, and I want him to be a doctor. Then I want the second to be a girl, and she should be a nurse. I want to take care of the children and send them to school, but I also want to work so that I'll have something to do.

The most devastating situation occurs when the girl finds her way to marriage blocked, not only because she has not yet found the man she dreams of, but because she is too aware of her own fear of marriage. These youngsters are not neurotically frigid— they simply have lived through the horrible realities of sexual abuse, of a torn home. These girls find no way into their future:

> I have no ambition. Everything is useless. I would want to have children but not a husband.

A pretty eighteen-year-old, intelligent but with no high school diploma, looks worried:

> . . . Mostly you know, everybody that gets married young always gets divorced. When I get married I want it to be permanent. But marriage doesn't interest me. . . . I don't really want any children, because I don't have . . . I have the patience with them when I'm watching them. . . . I like them, but I just couldn't be with them all day long for all the time. I just . . . like when my sister's kids were there, I just couldn't stand it all the time. The yelling and all that got on my nerves, and I couldn't take it. That's why I don't want to get married in a way, too, because I don't want children. I like them. I love them, but I don't want to have any, because if I had some, I'm afraid that I wouldn't be a good mother to them. That's the way I feel.

Two sixteen-year-olds—one an American Indian and the other from a German background—talk earnestly:

> Sometimes I think I might marry. There is Adam. But Adam drinks, and I said I would not marry him if he drinks. When I told him that, he stopped drinking and got a job. His mother thinks I am wonderful because he stopped drinking for me. He said he wouldn't drink anymore if I would just marry him, but when I was sent up here he started to drink again. Maybe I can help him, but I don't really know.

> I don't want a man who drinks and I don't want a man who beats me up. I want a man who is not too old and who has a good job and I don't care what kind of job. I think he should be kind and good.

By saying what she does not want, she expresses what she has experienced—too much.

We see that our deprived girls are actually still in the same position as working women before the time of emancipation. They feel forced into undesirable, low-paying jobs, and try to find their way out through marriage, but even this is often blocked by lack of opportunity or their own disastrous experiences.

Yet emancipation has had its influence, and it has deepened the conflict and the dissatisfaction. The girl no longer simply accepts her lot. She resents her position more than ever; she compares it with that of men. She usually does not realize that this places a difficult demand upon her: the demand that she prepare herself for a working life. She sees only the lack of equality and privilege. And some of the girls begin to question the right to "stereotype" occupations for women. The delinquent girl usually does not join organized activities to fight for a cause. She simply feels angry and hurt; she complains and takes revenge in her own way. Beautiful Anna has a history of prostitution:

> I'm dead tired on my feet in the evening when I do waitress work. And what do I get for it? I can make as much in one night as I make in a month doing that kind of work. But nothing else is open for me.

In the delinquency institution in which she was placed, no vocational counseling or training was available. The girls learned a little beauty culture and cleaned the cottages. This was the total amount of vocational incentive or "training." Most members of the staff had little imagination and not much knowledge about any other opportunities for girls. Confronted with rather spirited youngsters who are thirsty for adventure and need an outlet for their energies, but who have little motivation for schooling—though frequently very capable of it—they knew only how to preach "hard work and learning," but could not motivate them. Institutional personnel alone are not responsible for this situation. Most positions for girls—outside of those based on academic achievement—are still vastly underpaid, and society still discriminates against girls who seek out the more unusual occupations. "I wish I could be a truck driver. But they won't take girls for that," said a husky nineteen-year-old. She should drive a truck—she would do it well. Yet she was made to feel that this was very "unfeminine" and wrong. She, too, was steered into becoming a waitress. She continues to be "in trouble." She is very angry and resentful—and empty.

An eighteen-year-old began to tell me about her wish to be employed as a beauty operator or a nurse, but it sounded false. When she gained more confidence, she said,

> You mean I should tell you *really* what I want? But nobody wants to hear that! They will think it's absolutely silly. What I would like to do is to live among Indians, to take care of horses, to wear jeans and shirts and no silly girls' clothes.

She was made to feel guilty because of her lack of interest in the more feminine occupations. She began to feel more and more like an outcast, so she acted like one. She is now in a prison.

> Boys have it better. If they want to work hard, they work on the roads and they get then a decent pay. There is nothing like that for us.

This idea came from many.

There is no question that there are girls in our present society who have cut through prejudices in employment and who do the kind of work some of these girls would like to do. Yet these are only few, usually especially strong and secure individuals.

Aside from certain manual labor reserved for women, there are other occupations traditionally assigned to them: nursing, taking care of the weak. A large number of delinquent girls want to do such work. Behind their "tough" exterior, they yearn to help.

> I would like to be a nurse. . . . I want to do something to help Indians on the reservation. . . . I want to help Indians to be someone. If I am a nurse then I want to help with old people.

> I wish I could work at a children's home or in a hospital. I want to work with very little kids.

> I love to be around animals. I would like to go to college and become a veterinarian.

> I like animals very much. I would like to learn a lot about horses and then teach kids how to ride. I like to roam. . . .

> I want to work as a nurse for about three years. Then I want to get married and get the best for my children: an education, no

trouble, and a good father. I never want to punish my children. I know I must say *no* sometimes but I will never, never beat them.

The last was said by a sixteen-year-old Negro girl who has lived through many marital conflicts between her parents.

Unfortunately too often the girl will tell that she tried to find work in nursing homes or assisting with animals, but that each time the pay was exceedingly low. Many of those girls could give superb care and it is no secret that such care is desperately needed.

Recently minimum wage legislation has been passed to include some of the typical women's occupations.[2] Yet minimum wages do not take care of the fact that such hard work is still underpaid and that there is little opportunity for advancement.

High scholastic requirements for admission to the helping professions are very discouraging to girls who have little incentive or little tradition of going through a long period of schooling. Neither their families nor they themselves nor any other people in their environment have conditioned them toward it. Yet they could make a real contribution in many of the helper-starved services if there could be more flexibility in training them on the job. The desire of the girls is genuine, but needs support:

> I would like to work with kids, but I don't want to be a school teacher. I have only finished eighth grade, and I won't go on to school much longer. I would love to work with kids in a family and in a children's home. Kids are always different, and they are so sweet and kind.

> I would like to go to college and study social work and psychiatry. I know it is a long study. I will have to first earn a living for my baby, but perhaps I can take evening classes. I never thought that I was very capable, but they gave me some tests and they think that I am of superior intelligence. I don't know, but I sure would like to try some studies.

Perhaps because of her particular cultural background, the American Indian girl frequently hopes to work with old people because

[2] See Fair Labor Standards Act, as amended. This act bars wage discrimination because of sex. Minnesota Minimum Wage and Maximum Hour Laws for Women and Minors affect women employed in the following occupations: retail, dry cleaning, laundry, manufacturing, mechanical, public housekeeping, beauty parlor, restaurant, hotel, motel, boarding house, rest home, resort, and hospital (excluding nurses or other professionals) as well as women employed as telephone or elevator operators. Concerning the Fair Labor Standards Act, as amended, see "Fairer Wages for the Fair Sex," *Business Week*, No. 1814 (June 6, 1964), p. 74.

they are helpless. She often feels a deep affection for them. Many of these Indian girls also know the desperate need of their own community and want to improve it. Listen to two fifteen-year-olds, a Sioux and a Chippewa:

> I would like to be a nurse, but I am not sure that they take anybody who has been in the training school. I want to do something to help Indians on the Indian Reservation. . . . I want to help Indians to be someone. If I am a nurse, then I want to help with old people. I get along best with old people.

> I would like to work with old people. I once was at an old age home. I like to help them. If I can't do that, I would work with little kids, but I would like better to work with old people who can't do things for themselves. . . .

> I thought last night about what we talked about. I thought what I really wanted to do if I got out of here. I would like to go to the reservation and help the younger kids. Maybe I can play with them so that they have something to do. I know I must go through school to do that. I think I could learn. I am far back. Perhaps I can do two years in one year. I should like to try. . . .

Besides having to face racial and economic handicaps, the girl, once adjudicated delinquent—especially after an experience of removal from the community—feels stigmatized and becomes even more discouraged about the prospects of ever fulfilling some of her ambitions. You heard one say, "I am not sure that they take anybody who has been in the training school." This fear, repeated frequently, adds to more evasion of any attempt at trying to find gainful employment or to prepare oneself for it:

> I would like to be an airline hostess, but I have never been in a plane. I have written to the airlines, but they have never written to me. I guess they never take anybody who has been here.

This is not unrealistic. In spite of the juvenile court laws which were created to guarantee that these youngsters *not* be treated as criminals, we actually do treat them as criminals. This is exemplified in the terminology used: note the terms, *probation* and *parole*. The words "supervision" and "assistance" would be far more appropriate.

Certainly there are exceptions—girls who fight their way through in spite of community attitudes and other problems. These are mostly girls who have the good fortune to be endowed by nature with one of the assets highly valued in our time: good intelligence.

This fight is not easy, and they, too, will not succeed if they do not find people who give them help and support.

Ella and Pat may be fortunate in achieving their goal, but we cannot be sure. Ella, a very intelligent, tiny, serious fifteen-year-old with a sullen little face, disheveled hair, and nervously moving fingers, comes from a completely disorganized home—disorganized by alcohol and the father's desertion. The mother, who was not very bright, had difficulty understanding this strange girl. Also, sons had more meaning to the mother than daughters. When one of the boys was killed in an accident, the mother mourned him constantly, letting the girl feel that she was not wanted. The adults Ella met in her life usually seemed to her to act like her mother; this resentful little girl began to use her intellect to make them feel inferior. Instead of stimulating her, many of them tried hard to push her down, to make her feel less "uppity." So she began to search for a life that was more exciting, less uncaring:

> I have friends, some of the "good" kids, but they have such dull lives. They do nothing but go to school. . . . I don't know what one can offer except the excitement of stealing, but I think kids of my age should have some real job. That's more important.
>
> I have thought of a lot of things I want to be—a nurse, a mother, or an airplane stewardess, but right now I think I want to be a proofreader. How did I find out about that? I heard about it, and it seems that it would fit just right to me. I would like to work in a publishing house. I like to read and read, and have sometimes found mistakes in published material. I just read *The Scarlet Letter*, and I liked *Exodus* very much. I like to read about true things about people. Do you know *Sunshine and Shadows*? That was good too.
>
> It would be wonderful if one could make oneself really understood. Artists can. They write about people. I can't write my feelings on paper. So nobody can understand me. They really don't know. To really be understood we must not be shocked. They are always shocked about me. . . .
>
> I only wish people would try to understand the girls, but—girls should also try to understand grownups. I never understood my mother. . . . I don't want anyone to have to feel sorry for me. I want to go out and start new.

Perhaps Ella will be able to start anew.

I followed Pat a little longer than the other girls because of her unusual promise, but even now I am not yet sure that she will fulfill it. Pat sat next to me one day at lunch talking, like many of the other girls, about her boyfriend. Suddenly I heard her say, "We always fight about Schopenhauer." My mouth almost dropped open when I realized that she was talking about the German philosopher. When I asked more about it, she gave me a very accurate description of his basic ideas and where she differed from her boyfriend in regard to Schopenhauer's thinking. She was enchanted to find someone with whom she could discuss philosophy and she invited me to her room in the institution. She pulled out a dog-eared, obviously much-used history of philosophy in which she had underlined many passages. The young psychologist of the institutional staff had lent her his notes on lectures in philosophy and she had made careful excerpts of them. When I asked her how this interest had developed she told me that she had once heard the minister use the word "philosophy" and had been intrigued by it. She looked it up in the dictionary, was fascinated by the definition, and began to search for books on philosophy. No one had ever picked up on her interest. Once, when she mentioned it in school, a teacher made fun of her.

Who is Pat? She is one of a large number of brothers and sisters with an alcoholic father and a mother who has frequently deserted the family. Conditions in the home were always so bad that police or welfare officers were concerned. Everything was unkempt and in disrepair. There was always abject poverty. Pat was at times placed in boarding homes, returned home, sent to an aunt. When she ran away from some of the unpleasant situations, she was brought into court. Her behavior was always friendly. She complained only about school because she felt that she was not treated right. Her schoolmates knew that some of her brothers were in delinquency institutions and so did the teachers. She felt that everyone looked down on her and she could not stand this. It was significant that her dissatisfaction centered on the school, but nobody picked this up. This very gifted girl was hungry for learning but she herself did not know it.

Because of the unstable home life, she was sent to the delinquency institution without having committed any major delinquent act. This started Pat on the road to delinquency. After that, she was in and out of the institution for running away, keeping late hours, drinking, and, finally, for contracting a venereal disease.

I suggested to Pat that she read Kant, because of her struggle with values and Kant's basic approach to ethics. I sent her philosophy books and once received the following letter:

> I am still in school and studying my philosophy at every opportunity. My choice now is Immanuel Kant. I had some difficulty understanding his critique, but I enjoyed it very much at the second reading.

The office here has not sent the *Dialogues of Plato* over yet, but if you knew how thrilled I am to have it you would laugh. I look forward to getting it now.

I hope my letter finds you very well and happy. Of course, I know you are busy. So am I. I'm not in the honor cottage anymore. I guess my bitterness for the staff here has gotten me in trouble. I see no hope for parole, but I am content to be learning. . . . Maybe if you can think of some, you will jot down a little list of good books. You did give me one, but it was lost in a book. I would appreciate this more than I can say. You already know how rare good books are here at the school.

Pat's hope was to go to a university. Pat's innate intelligence measured by all available tests, in spite of her deprived background, left no doubt about her capacity. Yet, when I heard of her last, she had run away again. She could not stand the close association with so many girls. She became easily discouraged. Then she gave up the struggle. Pat increasingly defeated herself. There were perhaps too many long years of neglect behind her.

Pat, too, like many of the other girls, may not be able to find her way out of the narrow confinement of unfulfilled dreams. She does not accept this with suffering and passivity. She becomes more and more bitter and resentful.

Our present society postulates that women and girls should be regarded as active members who enjoy co-equal status with the male. Yet society still denies the female the opportunity of fulfilling this equal status. This rejection of a status of equality is one of the significant factors in precipitating the adolescent girl into delinquent behavior reactions.

A second factor that is part of the changing culture is the thwarted need for adventure. This need is an outstanding characteristic of adolescence in both boys and girls. In fact, it is sometimes the most outspoken one, stronger even than the sex urge. A fifteen-year-old once told me about her dreams of becoming a flyer and visiting jungles, and then added,

> I surely can't have that. I go out at night and neck with the boys, but I don't really care much about them. It's just something interesting to do.

Modern transportation has made the wish for adventure in the girl much more real. It has placed it into the realm of the obtainable. Yet, for the girl, restrictions on the fulfillment of this need are still much more limiting than for the boy. By tradition it was acceptable for a growing man to explore the world while the girl was supposed to stay at home. The old custom of the "Wanderjahre" in Europe allowed the male youth to roam freely across the country before he settled down to a job. No such outlet was available to the girl. This was accepted custom in past centuries, although individual women rebelled against the restrictions even then. The writer, George Sand, wore men's clothing and wrote under an assumed male name. The poetess, Droste-Hüdshoff, wrote of mounting a tower secretly, letting her hair fly in the wind, and dreaming of freedom and foreign shores. Today a girl can travel. Yet, even today, she cannot do this easily by herself. She often needs the boy to provide her with the means to fulfill her thirst for adventure. For example, it is more customary for the boy to have a car, which is the symbol of youthful independence in our time.

The girl from lower economic groups has always had to live in a rather narrow world. For centuries she has had to find excitement through quarrels and love-making. Yet today she sees the world on television. She wants to really live this adventure of life. Over and over the girls talked about their wish to travel:

> I know I will run away from here again, and so I will never get out. I want to be married, and not until I am about twenty-seven or twenty-eight. I want to have time, first, to go out and see things. I would like to travel to Hawaii and Europe. I have heard about those places, and I would like to know them.

> I would like to do something worthwhile to make up for what I did wrong. I would like to travel and see some of the world.
> I want to be an X-ray technician. One of my relatives is one and it looks good to me.
> Oh, I want to see the world and only then settle down. Much later, perhaps when I am twenty-five, then I may want to marry and have children.

The wide world has become so close, and travel posters make adventure seem possible. Crossing the oceans is no longer restricted to kings and queens, heads of state and their ambassadors; it seems within reach to all, but actually the cost of it limits it to those with sufficient money. Hurt and frustration are greater when something seems close, yet can never be reached. Drab and crowded city streets become even drabber. When the appetite is whetted by so much spice, blander offerings do not satisfy.

The third, deeply cutting area of cultural change is the uncompromisingly strict demand to put ideals into practice. This applies mainly to the demand for racial equality. Present times ask for more

than legislation. A new way of life, true integration without com-
promise, is something young people expect to practice. This is
reaching deeper into the personal life of each individual than it
did a hundred years ago.

On December 31, 1862, Abraham Lincoln received a letter from
the working men of Manchester, England. It is a document of a
burning wish to put principles into practice. They wrote:

> We joyfully honor you, as the President, and the Congress with
> you, for many decisive steps toward practically exemplifying your
> belief in the words of your great founders: "All men are created
> free and equal." You have procured the liberation of the slaves
> in the district around Washington, and thereby made the center
> of your Federation visibly free. You have enforced the laws against
> the slave-trade, and kept up your fleet against it, even while every
> ship was wanted for service in your terrible war. You have nobly
> decided to receive ambassadors from the Negro republics of Hayti
> [sic] and Liberia, thus forever renouncing that unworthy prej-
> udice which refuses the rights of humanity to men and women on
> account of their color.[3]

This cry for justice is the same today, but youth has become
impatient and wants to see it fulfilled now. Its implementation does
not remain on the level of public life; it does not concern solely the
working life of people. It reaches into social relations. Society must
come to terms with the demand that there be no claim to superiority because of the accident of skin color. Members of a generation
which has grown up accustomed to prejudice find it difficult to
free themselves from it, even if they want to. They frequently look
with fear or outright hatred at the young ones who not only claim
their rights or those of their friends, but who cannot even feel the
twisted emotions of race superiority.

When I asked youngsters whether they had any interest in public
affairs, I usually drew a blank. The girls I saw—most of them—
have little interest in politics and scarcely feel related to their
government. Yet almost all of them commented on the racial situation and that they thought it must change. Among the unmarried
mothers, who usually were in high school, graduates, or in college,
the issue was expressed more clearly and with less hostility than
among the delinquent girls, but it also showed deep personal concern:

[3] Letter to Abraham Lincoln, 1862, quoted in Henry Steele Commager, ed.,
Documents of American History, 5th ed. (New York: Appleton-Century-Crofts,
1949), p. 418. Reprinted by permission of the publisher.

I think about civil rights. I think the Negro should be accepted as citizens and should have all the rights. I feel the same way about Indians, too.

Politics don't affect me too much, and I don't think too much about it. Probably this is because I am not a colored person. I just don't think about it too much. I think a colored person should have just as much right in the United States as any white person, and if I were asked to defend a colored person, I would. We have no minority groups where I live.

I think the race problem is one of the important things of the day. Also Berlin and nuclear warfare are important. I think these three are the most important.

I think about the trouble down South and integration. I don't think it is fair. I believe in integration and that everyone should have just as much a chance as any other person.

And even more intensely:

My main area of interest is race relations. I have had occasional contacts at home. My father is in the military service, and all my life I have gone to school with Negroes and everybody else and no one seemed any different. We lived in the South for awhile and their attitudes were so completely different from those of the people I knew in the service! I suppose the contrast between them made me think.

There was a show on television . . . where a colored family moved into a new neighborhood, and I felt sorry for them and the way people did not accept them. I suppose because I lived in the South I feel as I do. I know it is not right. I can see the Negro's point of view. When someone is trying real hard, it is wrong to just push them back, and Southerners have pushed Negroes back so long, they have just given up. They just feel, "Where is it going to get me anyway?"

What is happening now down South I think is really wrong. At times, I would like to go down there and say what I think, but it wouldn't do any good. I think Negroes have just as much right to belong as we do. So many people you talk to—like my brother-in-law—are prejudiced. You don't get on the subject with him because he feels that strongly about it.

And I am against the way we treat Negroes. What would Abraham Lincoln say about what we are doing?

These girls felt a certain security, even if they disagreed with members of their own families, because they communicated with others and felt themselves a part of a total stream of new thinking and feeling.

The delinquent girl, in general, fights a private battle, as we saw in an earlier chapter, because of her essential loneliness and her inability to participate. She does not know that she is part of a changing culture; she sees herself only as an outsider, her feelings unaccepted. The "being in-between," the taking part in cultural change in all three areas—woman's position and work opportunities, outlet for adventure, racial integration—to her do not become a challenge in which she joins forces with others who move the wheels of practice and mores. Coupled with her isolation, changing values and contradictions weigh heavily on her and drive her farther into unacceptable behavior—unacceptable to her and to others. Yet she wants so much to be part of the "good" world, the community:

> I want to be back at age eleven and start all over again. I want to go to school. I want to finish and to be somebody. I want to have a good name and be a nice girl. . . .
> I wish there were somebody to help!

says a sixteen-year-old.

And her friend cries out:

> I just want to be like any other girl!

5. WAYS OUT
OF
LONELINESS

*"Behold, our days are so op-
pressed,
Our nights so full of
dread . . ."* [1]

Because the adolescent girl feels so essentially alone, because she must experiment, because she yearns to talk things over,
because she must try out her new strengths and her doubts, because
she must become part of a generation different from the one preceding her, because of all this, she needs desperately the association
with other adolescents. This applies to all adolescents, boys and
girls, even the comparatively happy and secure ones. Friendships,
group life, love relationships, take on major importance at this age
for all of them. If they are apart from others with whom they can
talk or try out their own thinking and their own feelings, they
cannot really know who they are. One cannot know whether one is
worthwhile if one does not have an experience of success with one's
contemporaries. One cannot know whether one is capable of making
a decision if one has not talked it over with others.

Yet, since these necessary group associations and real friendships
were usually out of reach for the girls I saw, they had to find other
outlets. Some withdrew, some fought the loneliness by legitimate
or illegitimate means. They had to do something about it because
a vital need was not fulfilled.

As long as the girl fights it or works through her loneliness she

---

[1] Rainer Maria Rilke, "Prayer of the Maidens," *Thirty-one Poems,* an English
version with an introduction by Ludwig Lewisohn (New York: The Beechhurst
Press, 1946). Reprinted by permission of the publisher.

is still healthy. She may become a nuisance to society and she will suffer, but there is a healthy spark which allows for change. The one who gives in to the loneliness, who ceases to fight, is the seriously disturbed one. Those are the girls who make suicide attempts or take drugs or who start the flight into mental illness. One of them described the beginning of this:

> I need understanding and a sense of belonging. You don't know how it is. There is no protection. All my life I can only remember drinking and fighting. I had "spells" when I was upset. I couldn't move but all the time I could hear. I could hear! I heard them fighting and fighting. When I woke up all I could do was to scream "Daddy, Daddy!" I couldn't express myself in writing or in poetry. The only thing I used to do was to draw trees and call them "Lonely." They are just bare trees, just bare!

The need to "belong" is as great as hunger and thirst. Yet to the youngster who already has problems—either because of belonging to a discriminated racial group or because of inner problems or because of difficult family relationship—the way to friendship groups is almost totally closed or the hurdles so great that she cannot take them. Parents do not want their children to associate with "those girls." The girls themselves feel awkward and unaccepted even when the outside does not reject them outright. Yet the people they feel most comfortable with are frequently forbidden to them. An Indian teenager said, "I have always felt so alone; I had no one. I finally found some friends here." "Here" was the delinquency institution where, for the first time, she felt warmth and acceptance by peers and learned to talk out problems with others. Yet she had to look forward to what another seventeen-year-old mentioned:

> When I got out of the delinquency institution, I continued my friendship with the girls I knew from it. That is violation of probation rules, but these are my friends! I knew it was violation but I thought I could get by with it. I *had* to!

The present practice of placing adolescents together in intensive living situations, of asking them to get along with each other, to share and learn to give and take, and then forbidding them ever to communicate with those who became close to them, intensifies the desperate loneliness and contradicts a normal impulse for friendship. The girls share in institutions experiences which are very significant to them. This experience is similar to that known in college dormitories or in military service. Yet the moment they leave the institution, they are not supposed even to recognize the friends they made in the institution. At the same time, the community in general refuses to open its arms to offer them new friendships. This is an impossible situation and leaves the girl feeling completely abandoned. In all the group sessions conducted with girls in institutions, the problem of friendship came up spontaneously whenever the girls spoke of "life on the outside." Here is an excerpt from a group discussion:

Alma. You know what's hard for a girl when she gets out . . . ; the rest of us know more or less the same people, and the same type of people in different degrees. It is hard to think, "Well, I'll give them up." You just can't give them up if you don't have anything to substitute with. You think they will never do you any good, they really deep down don't care about you, but you don't have anything else.

Bea. Well, you must get somebody else.

Alma. But, don't you understand? As long as you have these others, you can't get anybody else. Now, what do you have?

Anna. I don't think there are very many really true friends. Lots of acquaintances, but not friends.

Alma. I'm not strong enough to leave them. That's right. Because I don't want to be alone. And I have to have them. You can't just stop and say, "I don't want you for a friend." So you just go.

Bea. I'm going to go find myself some new friends!

Alma. You can't do that.

Anna. Because it takes a long time to find friends.

Alma. You can't go half-way. You can't go one night with the right people and one night with wrong people.

Bea. All the way or not. That's why it's hard for a girl from up here, because you can't cut yourself loose. They say, "Find some new friends." How? Lock myself up in a room and say "goodbye" to everybody? "I'm not going to see you anymore" and then go out on my own into a whole new world?

Anna. Because after you sit home for awhile and you don't know anybody, then you go out. Nobody knows you. Are you supposed to sit home always and read a book?

Alma. You either call up your girlfriends who have been up here or go to them. They don't care where you're from, what you did, because they're in the same place you are.

Anna. You can't call the others, because all they say is, "You're from the Delinquency Institution." You're no good, they think, because maybe *they* get a job. You have to always go to the other ones that don't have anything, and they'll take anybody into their crowd.

The last comment is the most significant one. The people who also feel that they "don't belong, that they don't have anything" are the only ones who are willing to take the "forbidden" girls into their circle. This crowd then becomes their home, although it does not fulfill completely their longing for a more significant personal relationship. It makes them feel that they are no longer outcasts and diminishes their terrible fear of being so totally alone.

When they describe what they are doing in the crowd, one is struck by the quality of anonymity, of their just being with others without any strong form of interaction: "I just like to sit there. I say nothing. I just spin the records." Or, "We do really nothing, we sit there. We listen to music. We may close our eyes. We sway to the music." The crowd wards off the deafness, the fear. It rarely involves the girl actively.

Only the gang is different. It demands action and participation. Yet the girls I met rarely belonged to gangs. Of the approximately 175 girls with whom I talked, only two spoke of belonging to organized gangs, and only one of these gangs resembled those discussed in the literature describing boy gangs in the large metropolitan centers. This girl described a gang with unusually cruel initiation rites, in which the youngsters were severely beaten. She had a family history of unspeakable brutality, and seemed to be proud of her immunity to pain. The other gang was a strange mixture of sophistication, naïveté, and delinquency. A description by Ella, a fourteen-year-old girl who belonged to this gang, showed a greater active involvement than did most other participants in "crowds." Ella showed many behavior problems at home and at school. She was a bright girl, but never achieved in school. When I sat down with her, as with all the others, and told her that she should feel completely free to say what she thought, that nothing would go into her record, that I was there to listen and to understand, her expression of distrust disappeared rapidly and she became exceedingly outspoken:

> Adults don't understand what we need. What I mean is that they cannot distinguish when there should be privileges and when there should be restrictions. They want to know where we are every minute. When I went out with kids and we decided suddenly we wanted to go to a drugstore or go sleigh riding, I always had to stop and call. And then this business of being at home on time!

It might be better to start half an hour early and then one can make it. Parents ground the kids for far too long when they have come home late even if it is just for being five minutes. Then in other things they are ridiculously loose; they don't seem to care. My family called the cops when I just was one hour late.

Observe here the general and typical adolescent complaint about restrictions, but also the astute observation of inconsistency, and especially the quick "reach" for outside force on the part of the family, instead of being able to handle the conflict in a more private manner.

In summer, they never let me go to the lake. I couldn't understand that. They said I should go only with the kids in my neighborhood, but there are only little kids. I just had a fit.

When I am with my friends, we just fool around. We dance, we don't do anything wrong. Most of what we do, we do just for fun. Once we jumped a boy and gave him a hickey only because he is so against it. We neck but it isn't serious.

My parents never gave me any sex information. All I learned, I learned from the boys, but it is sufficient. No, I certainly don't have intercourse. We just neck in a group for fun. We did it the other day in the basement, tight like in a telephone booth.

I belong to a gang. I don't belong to the Bluejays. They are called Bluejays because they dress sharp. They cut their hair short and wear tight, continental pants and tight shoes. Those are the rich kids; they can afford it. I belong to the Sparrows. They are the poor kids. Our leader is John. He is very handsome.

The girls go steady with the boys. You get into the gang for your personality. You have to be somebody who looks innocent but isn't. You should see John—he has the biggest, bluest innocent eyes.

People don't take it seriously when you love somebody. They call it puppy love. Kids are serious about affection. Juliet was only fourteen years old. My sister says you are just rationalizing. Well, we wouldn't be human if we didn't rationalize. We have brains. I don't know why we go steady. I know for me it isn't just to have security. I don't know. I can't explain it.

In our gang, we talk a lot about religion. All the kids with the exception of myself and one other girl are Catholics. Religion means most to all the Catholic kids. You see, they all went to parochial school and they hate that school, but religion still means much. They can be awful drunk on a Sunday morning but they always go to church. My foster father disapproves of this. He says that this is hypocrisy, but I don't think so. The Catholic Church approves of drinking and doesn't mind if you smoke. I think

Catholicism is the almost perfect religion. I may turn Catholic. I am reading right now, but I must discuss this more.

Many of the kids are also in an Air Force organization. It is kind of military. It asks for a lot of hard work and you wear sort of a uniform. I wanted to join but for me it is too much work and a bit too strict. Those kids also drink a lot. We like to drink. It is fun. *You see we try to be adults. We can't wait to grow up. We want to, because adults are a class by themselves. We are always in between. We don't like that.*

With my boyfriend, I discuss parents and problems at home. He wants to be my close boyfriend, but I am not yet sure. There are nine kids in that family. That is just too many. He wears the sharpest clothes. He wears those cool continental jackets. He wears tight jeans each time in different colors. He can afford it because he works twice a week in a bakery.

School—I hate it!! Why? One has to get up too early in the morning and everything is compulsory. One should have more time off. Actually we do have more time off than people who work, but we are young only once. School is so monotonous. They flunked me in ninth grade and I am repeating it now. It's so boring. When I tested, I tested everything on the eleventh or twelfth grade level, but they flunked me because I have the wrong attitude. Now I am more bored. The only thing I like is civics.

I want to be an attorney or a social worker. I think delinquents know better how to work with delinquents. We know how delinquents get rid of the cops. I don't want to get married until I am thirty years old. If you get married too young, you will be an old hag. I have one sister who has four children and she is pretty and looks like a fifteen-year-old. That's okay. I have another who got married at sixteen and she looks really like an old hag. She has no fun. I want to have fun first.

Our gang has fun also with fighting. Someone who crosses us, we take care of. Once a boy was hurt badly. We don't really want to harm anyone seriously, but they can't make fun of us.

Sure, we discuss issues. I think communism is terrible. We discuss that, but then someone says "It's God's will." They are so fatalistic. We were very upset when Kennedy got shot. We cried. It made everyone sick. I didn't like him or his politics, but I was sick when he was shot. There is no race issue among us. We have mutual respect, Negro and white. We don't look down on anyone. We do think about communism and nazism. How gullible can people be, and for that matter, intelligent people.

We are troubled because we are bored, bored stiff, and we also live in fear because you never know what parents want from you. I wish we knew where to draw the line. I think delinquents will make the better parents. Only perhaps one will be too harsh, because one knows all the tricks and the kids will not be good anyway.

We kids need a place where we can just sit and talk and smoke. The trouble is when we have a place like that, someone always does something that makes the adults angry and then we wreck things. Like once the boys put something into the laundromat and it flooded everything. Now we can't go there anymore.

One of the boys stole a radio. His parents right away called the cops. I think if they had just talked it over with us, the radio would have gone back and we wouldn't feel so resentful. Sure, we girls could influence them but sometimes we are too late in thinking about it.

Stealing doesn't bother us morally. But we don't steal from each other. I am terribly nervous when someone steals something. It bothers me. It bothers me even to drink. They say when you drink you forget. It is not that way with me. If I drink, I face reality. I blurt it out. There are things I forget but when I get drinking, I remember them. It's just the opposite with me.

I think it would be good to discuss problems with other girls. It is also good to have a third party that can listen.

I love my gang. We are not a bad gang, but there is quite a lot of stealing. I only once belonged to another group, but this was really stupid and that leader was just not worth anything. I am looking forward to coming to another group.

We see the rebellion but we also see the yearning for friendship, for being with others, for being "one of them," for fighting the adults, for gaining some affection, but also for thinking through serious problems.

Existing clubs and youth organizations seemed not to fulfill the needs of those girls who had gotten into severe difficulty. The girls felt that they were not acceptable in some of the groups— that the other girls there considered themselves "too good" for them—or they found the activities too childish.

Once I was part of a church youth group but it didn't mean much to me. I like to be with older people.

Before I started going with a wild group I went to some clubs in a center. I was at camp once but it seemed kind of childish after awhile.

Many of the youth-serving agencies seem to be geared too much toward girls with high leadership capacity and with a great deal of self-confidence. They also presuppose family involvement or family support, which is not available to many of the girls. They serve well the young child, but when adolescence approaches, their programs lose the interest of girls who need "spicier" adventure to allay their thirst for coming closer to a locked adult world which seems so full of mysterious satisfactions denied to them.

In these groups adult leadership was often as far removed from the girls' daily life as teachers in school. They spoke another language and had not enough skill to unlock sufficient trust, in order for the girl to admit her dependency needs. This same invisible wall existed also between them and their more privileged or less troubled contemporaries.

The first way out of loneliness for them is the *joining of a crowd*, a losing of themselves anonymously in it. While the crowd allays some of the feeling of emptiness and allows for some outlet of the need for adventure, it does not fulfill the yearning for a more significant, more intense relationship. We know that all adolescents are highly emotional and have strong mood swings. The girls I saw were especially so, in an introspective and unrealistic way.

The second way out of their loneliness was a highly romanticized love relationship. Their concept of boy-girl relationships was the sentimental one from the glamorous dream world of the movies. It seemed almost completely out of context with what they saw around them. When she came from a drab environment, full of quarrels and often abusive relationships between the parents, the girl pretended that her relationship to one boy was the greatest love relationship without any possibility of a conflict. The Cinderella story with its enormous contrast between the degrading and dirty reality and the marvel of the one-and-only Prince Charming seemed to be repeated in practically all of them. There was deep resentment against anyone who tried to destroy this picture. To them the boyfriend was the true lover, even if they knew that he was involved with other girls.

> Although he wasn't mine alone,
> Although his love I shared,
> A better man I've never known;
> For him I'll always care.
>
> Oh I know very well that he didn't love me;
> I know he had other girls too,
> But there isn't a man better than he
> And there's nothing for him I won't do.

The following poem was addressed by a seventeen-year-old to her boyfriend whom she knew to be promiscuous:

> Till death do us part, do you know what that means?
> As long as I live, there'll never be anyone but you.

And when the time comes, I pray I'll be the first
Cuz I couldn't live without you anyhow.

For richer or poorer, well that's no problem,
If I had all the kingdom in the world,
I'd still be poor without you;
And tho I'm poor . . . I'm the richest girl
In this world if I have your love.

For better or worse, well that's only a question
Which asks if I'd stick it out, if the going
Got rough. And all I have to think of
Is how rough it would be without you
And I know I could go thru anything, as long as you love me.

Till death do us part, in my arms, in my heart,
And with every breath I take, I think of you;
For me you're the reason every new day
Dawns, because I love you so much and always will,
Till death do us part. . . .

If she remembers at one point that the man is not exactly what she makes him out to be, she takes full responsibility for the disappointment upon herself. This same girl wrote:

Darling, I know it was I
Who said our last goodbye,
But when you left, I broke down and cried
For my heart was bleeding inside.
I'll never know what made me tell that lie
And whenever I recall it—inside I seem to die,
Wishing I could take back those words
That made your heart break in two,
To kiss and hold you near and whisper, "I love you."

If a break comes, loneliness seems almost to overwhelm the girl.

Neglect
(written by another seventeen-year-old)

Stop! Don't turn and go.
Don't leave me here to cry,
So all alone with not a soul
To help the time pass by;

Yet every night you say goodbye,
A kiss and nothing more,
You leave me once again to cry
Behind my silent door.

Oh many a night and many a day
I spend here in despair,
But you go on in the same old way
As though you didn't care.

If only you'd spend a little while—
Perhaps an hour or so—
To talk with me and make me smile . . .
But, no, you have to go.

Love, never mind my foolish thoughts
I'll keep them to myself
Besides—I'd rather be unhappy with you
Than happy with someone else.

A Lesson

(written by the same seventeen-year-old)

I've traded love for agony,
My joy has turned to fear.
My friends are now my enemies
My smiles now are tears.

For it was I who knew so much,
And thought I'd tell the world,
Instead it turned and spat on me
A lost and lonely girl.

Don't doubt that I have learned from this.
I always use my head.
Tonight I'm going to kill myself—
I'll be better dead!!!

In the boy-girl relationship, many girls are willing to take a great deal of abuse. In several of the group meetings in the reformatory the eighteen- and nineteen-year-olds discussed the problem of having been beaten by their lovers. Some insisted that it was better than having nobody, while others began to rebel against this treatment and said that they would never again let a man hit them. The terrible need of having someone close at any price drives the girl to expose herself for long periods or repeatedly to mishandling:

Loving you like I do
Has taken me but one step from hell.
Whoever said that love is beauty?
Beauty is happiness.
And never in my love for you
Have I found a moment's happiness.

And I am damned!
Why must I go on, only to take that final step?
Why?
Because nothing in life means more to me
Than loving you like I do.

(a seventeen-year-old)

The delinquent girls' disregard of reality in the love relationship was far more outspoken than for other girls, including those I saw in the homes for unmarried mothers. The unwed mothers, too, spoke of the adolescent yearning for closeness, but they were more aware of their boyfriends as real people. Many discussed with them in a mature way the responsibility for the coming child. Several of them had consciously entered sex relations because of a code they shared with most of the present adolescent population, namely, that sex relations are permissible if one is in love, while reprehensible when love is absent. In spite of their adherence to this code, many felt guilty and had not been happy or satisfied while having intercourse. They felt that they had to give in to strong pressure from the boy to prove their love.

The incidence of what may be called "emotional rape" seems high. It is a combined persuasion and pressure exerted by the boy with strong emphasis on making the girl feel that she is harming him if she does not give in to his desire. She is pressed to prove her love, to not be "a prude." The appeal also is made to a sense of sacrifice in the girl, a mixture of maternal feelings toward the boy, of submissiveness, and also of desire. The latter is often not very strong, but individual persuasion and the group mores of the prevalent code press hard on the girl. In general, she is able at some point in the relationship to assess her partner as a real person.

In contrast to this, the delinquent girl held on to the illusion of some idealized image, with the exception of those few who had become unable to establish any kind of meaningful relationship. Only those few came close to the stereotype of the delinquent as generally promiscuous.

When the girls had time to think, to share their disappointments and thus to overcome some of their unreal romanticism, they struggled hard to come to an understanding of what a love relationship means, can mean, and should mean. Listen to a group discussion among older adolescents with a long history of delinquency, especially sex delinquency, behind them. They had been talking about the problem of having a child out of wedlock and about their wish to get married.

Bertha. All right, I have asked this question before, and I haven't gotten an answer from any of you. Like I wrote Father Brown and I told him, I said, "Sure, there is a woman here that I love very much, just like a mother. There are girls I love just like sisters. But I want to know what is the true love between a man and a woman?"

Rita. Hey, let's go around the table and everybody say it.

Bertha. All right, put it this way: what is your true meaning of love?

Rita. What does the word "love" mean to you?

Bertha. And how do you think love should be returned, when you give it?

Rose. I think love is understanding—

Bertha. Wait a minute. Don't anybody interrupt her. Just say what you say when it's your turn.

Rose. You just interrupted me.

Bertha. No, no, I mean if somebody don't agree with you.

Rose. I think love is sex, understanding one another. (*sigh*) I don't know. It is so many things.

Lisa. Well, I will tell you what I think it is. No, I don't know whether any of you . . . . Oh, there are a few of you that know this. I honestly do think I am in love with an older man. I'm going to give it some time and consideration. But to me the real meaning of true love is where you can talk things over with him. You can be completely truthful with each other without having to beat around the bush or lie to each other. And for each one to be able to understand the other one, and if you do not understand, at least try to see their side of it. Well, certainly sex has a big part to play in it, but I don't think it's completely all of it. And, well, if something comes up, like a girl getting in trouble and where the boy has to wait—if he really loves the girl, I mean, he can—maybe he hates her for the things she does, but yet he is willing to forgive and wait and give her another chance. I also think that a real true love is where you can meet problems together. Anything that comes up, you can always be behind each other. It is more or less just understanding. Well, I think it is giving and taking equally. That's what my opinion is. Maybe I'm wrong. But that's the way I feel about it.

Dora. I feel pretty much the same way as she does. I mean I have the same ideas and everything. Because to me, true love is something that is shared by two people, and it has to be on both sides. Not just one party. And you have to know and understand each other and to learn each other's faults and try to help each other.

Rita. To me, love is giving of yourself. If you love a man, you give him understanding, compassion, give him the feeling of being needed. If I loved somebody I would give myself to him in every way that he needs me or every way that he wants me. It's to give. That's the way I feel about it—just to *give*. It's not to *get*, it's to give. When you give yourself, you get. You get, no matter how little you give, you get something in return. If you give love, you're going to get it.

Peggy. I think that I agree mostly with what Lisa said. It's just a whole lot of things, not just good things, but bad things. It's being able to cope with them equally and not to try to ignore the bad, but to understand it and be able to talk it out. Oh, I don't know.

Rose. I think there should be fights once in awhile too. That's the best part of understanding.

Bertha. Now I could be wrong too. My true meaning of love is: I have found love twice, but when he loved me, sure, I loved him; but he was married. The first one was married, and I got sick of it after five years. I mean, sure, I had gone with other boys and at times—there were times when he and I would go back together again. And the other one I still love very much, and he says he loves me. Sure, but what is love if you go around forging checks together and having sex together? He wanted to marry me. He and I were going to go down to my parole agent. He wanted to marry me. He wanted to accept this child. It is not his child. My true meaning of love is this: You not only give, but you have to take too, and you share the family, the joy of having children, the joy of being married, and I believe you should go to church. I'm not that much of a person for church, but I believe in time it will come. I believe being of the same faith and talking your problems out together and trying to figure out where you have failed and how you can keep up and go on without ending in the same way. If I could find somebody to meet my ends the same way I do, then, like Dr. Gill [a psychiatrist] said, I would marry for life. I would never have a divorce. When

I was a child, and I used to go talk to him he used to say, "Bertha, what is your dream about marriage?" My biggest dream was holding my first child in my arms, and I never dreamed that it would be out of wedlock. But . . . some day I don't know when, or how old I will be, there will be a man come along who will accept my infant, and they will meet, and I'll be happy.

The thoughts expressed are similar to any value system in regard to love and sex among nondelinquent adolescents. In fact, they are rather conservative. The assumption that they have talked this way because of the presence of the group worker is not valid, because these particular group discussions were conducted by the researcher and the girls knew that nothing of what they said would influence their record. They had previously talked freely about very unacceptable practices and desires. Those were their actual feelings. The pressure of institutionalization accounts partially for them. They also represent the dream of being "respectable," and again the desperate wish of the adolescent to be part of an acceptable group. The conventional value system is an honest one, although reality involves a deep struggle with the incredibly sordid experiences they have behind them, the pressures of the world around them when they are outside of the institution, and their own drives and lack of other satisfactions.

When the girl is institutionalized, her need for romantic physical closeness is often transferred to her association with other girls.

All adolescents show attachment to those of their own sex, as well as to youngsters of the other sex. This is normal. The affection for other girls was stronger in the institutionalized ones.

> Most girls here go with girls. Some do it on the outside. This place here changes girls to the worst. They learn from each other, and it makes them feel so bad that they have been here. If you don't want to go with a girl, then they make you feel lonely.

> When I look at a girl . . . There's something about her . . . you don't even notice if she's pretty or not. She has something that just shines through, you know. It's something that is just like a magnet. It just draws you to that person. And if she looks at you and sees the same thing, you draw yourselves to each other. . . .

> Sometimes you find a girl, that . . . you want to have friendship but you want to have love, too. You want to live with this person. You want to . . . just outright, mature love. You want to help these persons, do things for them, be with them all the time, cry with them and laugh with them, share everything with them, their misfortunes, their happiness.

There is no question that confinement to a one-sex institution at a time when drives are especially strong partially accounts for this. Yet this explanation is too simple. The deeper reason lies again in the girl's feeling of being alone, and she cannot cope with this. There are other reasons for preferring love relationships with girls to those with boys. There is the girl who feels little self-confidence and considers herself ugly and undesirable. She does not dare to compete with others for boys.

> Oh, you must have heard about how girls get "queer." I don't think that most of them are really homosexuals. There are a few, and they can be known easily. I now have nice clothes which I never had. . . . Some girls are spoiled and get a lot from their parents, and some have nothing and get things from the welfare. My parents wouldn't send me a piece. Nothing. Now I have some things, because I "go with girls." That's one way of getting them. But I think that's only *one* reason why girls go with girls here.
>
> Maybe it's also because there are no boys around, but I don't think that's the main reason. I think it's because a girl is lonely, and that way she feels accepted.
>
> And there are many girls like myself who don't think that a man will ever look at her, because they are so ugly and nothing worth looking at. So it makes you feel good that somebody thinks you are something. If a man laughs at you, it's terrible! So, you are afraid of meeting men, and you go with girls.
>
> It's parents who make you feel low. My mother has always said that I am ugly. And then, if you are on the outside, and you are not pretty, kids laugh at you and tease, and that makes you worse. You hate the world. If finally somebody loves you, and if it is a girl, you are happy.
>
> I don't know, but right now I just feel content. I go with girls. Somebody loves me. . . .

In such a love relationship the girl feels some sense of worth which she had never experienced otherwise.

> If I look at me I can't imagine that anyone else would want to look at me. I seem so old to myself. . . . The girl I love looks so, so beautiful, I simply can't describe it to you. I never in my life thought that something as pretty as this could love me. I was so flattered. It made me feel like a new person.

And there is the girl to whom sex is something dirty and disgusting. She is afraid of the male, who to her seems brutal and threatening. To her, sex relations with a man may also be an act which can produce an unwanted child. To such a girl Lesbian activity is either a safer outlet or seems a form of higher love. In one of the group discussions the girls wondered how they could ever find "decent men" who would want something more than just "sex" from them. One of them dryly suggested that it was simpler to live with girls and get their satisfactions this way. They would have fewer problems to struggle with. Another one expressed her anger and rebellion against society which looked down on Lesbian practices. She insisted that to her it only meant tenderness and an increase of her better self:

> I have a girl, a simply wonderful girl. . . . I need her, I love her. I feel that we belong together. . . . It does good things for me. I feel better toward all people. I feel satisfied. Now I have somebody to care for. Now I have somebody whom I want to make happy and somebody I will work hard for. . . .

There is also the girl who enters homosexual activities mostly out of a sense of frustration and disappointment, almost as a form of revenge against the lover:

> I have erased all trace of you
> From both my heart and my mind.
> I search for new things to pursue
> I seek out love amongst my kind.
>
> I have erased you from my mind
> And put aside all thought of you
> Though sometimes in the night I find
> The old desire leaps forth anew.

Many of the girls struggle with their bisexual drives and they are not sure which way to turn. Rarely can they talk freely, because every expression of their doubts, fears, and desires in this particular area may be held against them. The punitive laws against homosexuality and the horror and disgust connected with it make it impossible for the girl to seek help. She cannot approach her social worker, psychologist, psychiatrist, or teacher because she knows that they have the power to deprive her of freedom or privileges—and she herself expects punishment, even for her thoughts.

It is known that illness cannot be treated if the patient deliberately prevents the physician from knowing about it. Yet this is frequently the position into which the girl is forced in her battle with the problem of Lesbianism. Fear of retaliation and shame close her off from any effective help. This is true also when her activities are known, or when they become an open status symbol —as is sometimes the case in large one-sex delinquency institutions. She then may boast about her girlfriends, her role as "butch" (the male) or "femme" (the female), but she still will not share with anyone in authority her conflicting desires, her fears, her elation, her self-doubts and self-accusations as well as fierce loyalties and depth of attachment. In such a case the problem itself is known, but nothing of its extent or the true meaning it has to the particular girl. The inner terror is usually only increased by institutionalization, with the result that the girl is then in contact with women only and without any recourse to heterosexual stimulus. Unfortunately many delinquency institutions, especially those for girls, are almost exclusively staffed by women, who have few satisfactions in their personal lives. They become "nagging mothers" and show frequently an exaggerated suspicion of any kind of friendship between girls, interpreting any kind of touch as a sexual one. Their harsh prohibitions drive the girls deeper into a territory that means more segregation from the "normal" society and feeling of worthlessness. (It must be understood that there are also excellent delinquency institutions where none of this occurs. For instance, those run by the Order of the Good Shepherd provide deep understanding, a good program, and sound professional help. There are, unfortunately, still too few of such institutions.)

The two major ways out of loneliness—the crowd and the love relationship—give only temporary relief to the girls. They do silence the pain for a little while, but basically they increase the estrangement, make the wound deeper, increase the hurt. A warying and insidious cycle continues: the girl feels abandoned—frequently she really is abandoned—searches for friendship, becomes abandoned again, or abandons others, because she cannot hold on to people, is being disappointed and disappoints others. And in this process she loses herself more and more.

6. INCREASINGLY LOW SELF-IMAGE

"And you who are seed,
and you who have in you
the hope and the creed
of new trees and
new branches,
new leaves and new gold
You—waiting to grow . . ."
Ruth Peiper (unpublished)

"Self-respect, the survival of the soul," said Spranger. Self-esteem is the ingredient which gives dignity to human existence. It grows out of human interaction, of being appreciated for what one is. It takes a long life of security to be able to say, "I know what I am regardless of what others think of me." And even the adult who has reached this stage has times of self-doubt. He needs renewed confirmation of his worth—either through some form of success or an act of love and kindness coming from someone else. Children are totally dependent on being loved, accepted, cherished; otherwise they cannot develop. During World War II, Anna Freud found that the children evacuated from their homes and separated from their parents suffered much greater emotional shock in a bomb-safe environment than those who stayed with their mothers during the bombardment. The latter experienced fear and pain, but the protective warmth of the beloved adult prevented more serious damages. They felt important by sharing those dangers with the adults. Being important to someone is a most necessary nourishment of the human spirit. Satisfactions are enhanced, when the child does something that adults appreciate. It means much to a child to hear the exclamations of approval when he takes the first step or says the first word. Self-confidence and assurance grow with other small accomplishments: the child starts to read, the child brings home a good grade, the child can recite a poem. Someone who praises is there, is happy with him. Many of the girls I saw had had no such childhood experiences, had never known the meaning of success. Some girls could not remember anything of their childhood—perhaps because it was too painful. They had never received praise for anything they had done. Many could only remember beatings and scoldings for the things they had done wrong. It was conveyed early to them that they were less than important, that they were a nuisance. Unfortunately, most of these girls experienced an additional decrease of their self-esteem when they entered school. The majority of the girls had at least good average potential intelligence, yet most of them had severe school problems.

School frequently had little relationship to their life at home. Expectations of teachers were often completely foreign to the girl who came from a home where learning was considered unimportant, imposed by strangers one feared but did not respect. The world of the school had absolutely no contact with the world of the home. Schools presented a life of books, of writing, of orderliness, while at home one never saw a book and order was unknown. A thirteen-year-old girl said:

> All I wish for, is once to finish a book. When I take a book out of the library I want to read it but there is so much noise around me at home that I read it too slowly and then the time is up and I have to give it back.

But who was aware of her wish? She only got scolded for not finishing her book.

> We never had any breakfast before we went to school.

Hundreds of youngsters in our comfortable cities go to school without breakfast, bring no lunch, and return to no prepared dinner. Some get free lunches in school, but many do not. Yet at school they are supposed to be alert. Since they are not and cannot be wide awake, they fail again.

The great emphasis on competitive grades in our schools and the increasing and pervasive high valuation of college add to the problem of the girl who—for many reasons, not only intellectual limitations—cannot and will not enter college. School gives little satisfaction for achievement in any other area. The non-verbal girl rarely finds opportunity for successful accomplishment. Art and domestic skills are not highly considered by the schools. I found that many girls in the institution blossomed out when they were allowed to use art media, especially paints. Girls seemed rather gifted in this area. It gave them a rare opportunity to express their feelings without being censored and it did not make high demands on verbal skills. For many, painting gave for the first time a feeling of accomplishment, some recognition of their being able to do something that deserved praise. The early and continued absence of any experience of accomplishment had made them feel totally inadequate and increased their essential isolation.

Being alone is not the same as being lonely. There are people who are alone, but they have an inner richness and a calm confidence in themselves which does not make them feel outcast, even if they are not among other people. The girls were so lonely that they felt separated from all others. The anxious quest of them—at least of most of them—was: "Do you think we are different, really bad?" They hoped so much to be reassured. But even a positive answer could not change their own feeling of being so very unworthy.

It is not uncommon for adolescents to feel "low," unimportant at times. Their moods swing sharply from peak to peak, from excessive self-confidence to dark self-depreciation. Frequently their daydreams of grandeur and heroic deeds are compensations for low self-esteem. A fourteen-year-old boy confided, "I dream of wanting to be Al Capone or Albert Schweitzer." The content of his ideal was not important. What he needed was to be "somebody." These common adolescent feelings of inferiority and self-doubt were especially strong and pervasive in the girls. Again, much of the feeling of inadequacy hit deeply into their total being as *women*. In our general culture success and "being somebody" mean for the girl being attractive and acceptable to boys. The less recognition she can achieve in any other area, as school or family or neighborhood, the more she must try to gain prestige through a love relationship. If she does not succeed, her self-concept sinks lower and lower: "I'm no good. I guess I never was good." In a sentence completion test one girl said it stronger and with finality: "I guess I'm just no good and never will be."

A very intelligent and gifted seventeen-year-old with the same complete distrust of herself moved from one sex relationship to another, increasingly despairing of her own worth as a person and of ever finding happiness. She expressed her losing fight in a poignant poem:

The broken and withered limb
Struggles, grasping, fighting to live
And doing so destroys the tree,
Its roots and all the blossoms it has to give.

The bent and twisted branch,
Grasping toward the light,
Sucking the life from its mainstay
Rather than becoming whole
Only, destroys all that to which it is connected.

I, like that bent and broken limb
Am unable to mend my broken ways,
But sucking, drawing, hanging on
Like a parasite to that which is pure and good.

Eventually that, too, will be broken
And without joy or blossom
Even as the limb fights to survive.
In doing so, it may destroy that which is good!
Shall I let go?

Self-hate is intensified by great unrelieved guilt. Guilt in itself is
not damaging. Guilt is one way in which conscience makes itself
felt. Guilt is a constructive force and can help a person to remake
his life if he sees a way of changing it. Guilt is destructive, however,
when it tears down the total person, when one sees oneself as completely bad, so that there is no strength to undo anything. If one
sees no redemption, one must either die or continue to live and
feel worthless.

I live in a house called torture and pain,
It's made of materials called sorrow and shame.
It's a lonely place in which to dwell,
There's a horrid room there, and they call it Hell.

From the faucets run tears that I've cried all these years,
And it's heated by my heart made of stone.
But the worst part to face is
I'll die in this place—
And when I die I'll die all alone.

The sad-eyed sixteen-year-old girl read this poem to me in a
monotone as if she wanted to avoid the impact of the feeling. A
few months earlier she had tried to commit suicide. Her stays in

delinquency institutions had been frequent. She did not often share her poetry. She seemed almost afraid of it. In writing, she sometimes found relief from the pent-up despair, but at other times it increased it.

Suicide attempts are frequent and usually are not "fakes." The girl seriously wants to destroy "something bad"—herself. Her guilt is so pervasive that she sees no hope. Nineteen-year-old Rita had also tried to commit suicide a few months before she came to the therapy group. She continued being depressed and was often cynical during the first sessions. During the time she was with this group, she learned that her child, who had been placed in a foster home, had died of a childhood disease. Fortunately, the support she gained in the group helped her to live through this without a new attempt at ending her life. She, too, found some outlet for her feelings in writing poetry which shows not only grief, but also the unhappy conviction that she is completely, and therefore totally, responsible for the death of her child. To her it is a punishment for her sins.

> When I was young I loved many;
> Now my days and nights are cold.
> Through the bad things of life
> Came a gift of light:
> A baby for me to hold.
> But I wanted still wild men at will
> And gave my son no name;
> And now he is dead, the ground for a bed,
> And my soul let it burn in flame.

* * *

> I knew a little boy
> He was my pride and joy,
> Born in a country town.
> He had a raven's hair
> And eyes, a black so true,
> But a heart that never I found.
> My son he was, but mine he'd never be.
> My heart shall it ever be free?
> I let him go for pleasures I wanted greater,
> Now I'm the one who has become the baby-hater.
> He died without me and so he'll always be.
> To hell I will go and for always I'll know
> How sinful a mother I be.

*   *   *

I have always lived and I always must,
But, why, I ask, now that my hurt has come.
My hurt—my son; he's now dust;
I'll never touch his hand; he'll never have a name.

Millions of babies have come and gone,
But only one held my heart in his hand.
His life, it passed like the night with the dawn,
Now he has his home in that far-off land.

Yes, I've always lived and always I must;
My son is gone and my hurt will go too far;
I forgot how to love, and no one do I trust,
Couldn't I die of feather and tar?

My baby was buried as babies are;
His body has changed from flesh to dust;
His heart has gone to be among the stars;
He never did live, but why? When *I* must?

*   *   *

My hand, a hard white pavement;
My heart, a brick of stone;
All dull dark streets like prison
From which all love has flown.
I need no man, no baby,
No one to love,
For I am made of little fakes I hate—
I do not love.
I'll take the little bypaths
With many a twist and bend
That reach way out
And find their end.
I don't want the stars and sun;
Nor I, the wind and rain;
I lost my love and I *found hate*.
I'll never love again.

*   *   *

He died, a baby in the night;
He died without a name
Because of his mother's flight.
She'll live for many a tortured year,

But death she never will fear.
She is wise to the price she must pay
So she will cry every night and each day.
She will suffer in hell by the flame.
Her son—he died, a baby in the night;
The baby she never held tight.

*   *   *

I loved this, but not now. Oh why?
I live my life in a hurting daze.
My heart is still—I feel it cry;
My sinful ways I can't deny—
I must go to hell ablaze.
To kill this hate now I must try—
But all I see, is a fiery haze.

We see the despair, the certainty that there is no way out for her, the feeling of being condemned, of having condemned herself. Being "bad" is total. There is no self-pity, because she feels that this condemnation is deserved. Punishment is expected, but it gives no relief, it does not help to expiate guilt. The girl not only feels guilty, she feels she is guilt incarnate.

Such pervasively low self-image seems to exist more in girls than in boys, even delinquent ones. One of the reasons for this is the fact that her self-concept is totally bound to her acceptance as a woman. Another additional factor is a general cultural image of what a girl should be. It is still "sugar and spice and everything nice." The ideal of a girl—and this is as deeply ingrained in girls as are the expectations placed upon them—is to be somebody kind and good and beautiful, and especially non-aggressive. When a girl becomes delinquent, she is overwhelmed by the discrepancy between what she should be and what she is, not only as an individual, but as a representative of her sex.

The girl in our culture finds less acceptable means for her drive toward aggression than does the boy. Being aggressive in itself is considered "unfeminine" and therefore wrong. Some sublimated aggression is permissible, as in some competitive sports or in intellectual endeavors, though here, too, are restrictions. The girl who lacks high skills or intelligence finds few acceptable forms of aggression. Her outlets become petty and destructive as nagging, hair pulling, gossiping. These behavior forms are despised by the girls themselves. They have none of the glamour of male aggression, e.g., fighting. This rejection of aggression marks a significant difference in the characteristic of the delinquent girl as compared with the delinquent boy, and adds to her self-depreciation. William Kvaraceus said that one can make one generalization about *all* delinquents:

> Here is where one of the rare positive statements about all delinquent behavior can be made: It is remarkably aggressive. Aggression may be verbal, it may consist of destructive acts, it may be sexual. Aggression may be directed towards one's self, towards the world, or both.

Kvaraceus preceded this statement by saying that

> In the broadest sense, any adolescent who is unsure of himself can appease his worries—or will try to—by being aggressive.[1]

This behavior is universal, but the problem for the girl is the fact that since aggression in itself is considered bad, it is forbidden to her. When a boy fights, he may be considered delinquent, because of the *form* in which he fights or the weapons he uses or the people he attacks. But his role in society does not prohibit fighting per se. On the contrary, the prevailing mores consider fighting part of the accepted male role.

Girls handle this problem by a subtle disguise of the aggressive act. Unconsciously many protect themselves against harsh self-censure by avoiding open aggression. Most of their sexual misconduct is a "passive one." The active soliciting prostitute was comparatively rare in this youth population. Stealing is a form of aggression, but not a violent one. Check forging, usually done only by the older adolescent girls, does not involve direct attack on a person. The few girls who had actually committed a robbery or assault found this offense not only unacceptable in the eyes of the law but in their own eyes:

> We robbed this gas station together. We both did not want it but what can you do if you have nothing? You could not beg! But I hated to see this poor guy suffer. I hate myself for doing something like this.

(As an aside, I want to point here to another interesting sign

[1] William C. Kvaraceus, "Juvenile Delinquency: A Problem for the Modern World," *Federal Probation*, XXVIII: 3 (September 1964), 15. Reprinted by permission of UNESCO.

of the impact of general cultural values. I questioned the girl about why she had so completely dismissed the idea of asking someone for help when they were destitute? She had used the word "beg" with deep scorn. She was surprised at my question. To her, *asking* for something—"begging"—was deeply degrading. Robbing meant doing something for oneself, it fitted better into the prevailing value of "rugged individualism.")

There was no boasting of direct assault on a person. When a girl had committed this, she usually did it as a helper to a boy or because she was, in her mind, under unusual stress. In the only two cases in which girls had pulled a knife against a person, the knife was not really used. In group discussion this kind of behavior was especially condemned. No girl defended violent actions, though they were willing to defend their right to steal or to some other misbehavior. A seventeen-year-old talked calmly about robbing someone, but direct aggression was abhorrent to her:

> If we don't have money, we rob people. I helped. I knew the boy we robbed. I had gone with him. He was a show-off. He always talked about how much money he had.
>
> Did I think about whether he had worked for it? Oh, you don't think of that! You just think you need money. What did I want and need money for? Clothes . . . , but I never bought clothes. I just drank. I used the money for drinking.
>
> I felt kind of sorry for him when the man I was with slugged him, but we took his billfold. I can do that only when I am drunk; otherwise, I would feel too sorry for him.

Another one showed the close connection between aggression and wishes for self-destruction:

> My boyfriend is now in the penitentiary. He got three to fifteen years for armed robbery. Why did we do it? We were desperate. We had had nothing to eat for two days. We actually never used the guns we had. We never took them into the place we robbed. We had them only in the car.
>
> *We wanted to kill ourselves,* but we had no chance. We didn't want to kill anyone. I was so afraid when we went into the building. We both were so afraid. I know he was.

No acceptable outlet for aggression, no way to relieve the guilt stemming from behavior they themselves despise, no hope of ever regaining a sense of self-worth, little or no sense of being protected, essential loneliness—all these increase the self-hate. But the destructive process does not stop with this. It is known that people who have little or no self-respect find it difficult to respect others. Hatred turns against others, individuals and groups. The degraded ones find their victims.

In spite of this knowledge, treatment of delinquents not only has taken little cognizance of this fact but often deliberately increases the feeling of degradation. In many girls' institutions, practices seem as if taken out of a textbook for purposely increasing the sense of worthlessness. In some of these places, simple adornment, including such culturally accepted practices as permanent waves or lipstick, are forbidden, thus making the girl feel more ugly, more undesirable.

Girls kept in solitary confinement in bare cells are not allowed to dress. They have no comb or brush. They sit for days on a mattress with nothing to do, nobody to talk to, stripped of everything that can make them feel human. Under such conditions girls become exceedingly bitter, close to suicide or thoughts of murder. They are cut off from human communication and made to feel base. Morris West, in speaking of the young priest who had been a political prisoner, writes:

> He had been beaten often but the bruised tissue had healed itself in time. He had been interrogated till every nerve was screaming and his mind had lapsed into a merciful confusion. From this, too, he had emerged, stronger in faith and in reason, but the horror of solitary confinement would remain with him until he died. . . .
>
> The nearest I came to losing my faith and my soul was when I lay naked and solitary in an underground bunker. . . . When I was brought back to the huts, to the sound of human talk—even to the sound of anger and ribaldry and blasphemy—it was like a new promise of salvation. . . .[2]

Even the highly motivated person, the person who is willing to accept suffering for an ideal, feels degraded and abandoned because of the segregation from any human being. How much more does this apply to those who have not chosen a certain way of life and to whom the suffering is not part of a conscious decision. Beyond this, these adolescents, close to childhood, are both vulnerable and in need of protection as well as being already filled with anger and despair.

Girls' institutions often increase the low self-concept by a whole

[2] Morris L. West, *The Shoes of the Fisherman* (New York: William Morrow & Co., 1963), pp. 17, 80. Copyright © 1963 by Morris L. West and reprinted by permission of the author.

design for daily living conducive to the wiping out of individual worth: by harsh regimentation, by giving little opportunity to the girls to make any decision, by making it impossible for their voices to be heard, by forbidding communication with friends, by treating the girls as inherently bad, exemplified in the comment of an employee of such an institution, "I'm always glad when I can go home to decent people." Another one shouted, "Don't tell me that you have not taken this. Once a thief always a thief, once a thief always a thief."

Some institutions have rules which imply something sick or vile in the girls, such as girls not being allowed to fix each others' hair, to touch each other, to speak to each other in a low voice (implication: homosexuality); girls must wear heavy long skirts even in summer (implication: being oversexed); girls are not allowed to talk during meals (implication: plotting some mischief). One could continue this list. In too many delinquency institutions, the whole atmosphere—the total program—undermines or destroys the already tenuous self-esteem. The girl becomes hopeless and gives up any attempt to change:

> You may laugh at me. I can't really talk with people, because I am sure they will laugh at me. If I say the truth about how I feel, what else can they do but laugh at me? I wish I could understand myself. I wish I could stop myself. I wish there was somebody that could tell me what I am or what could become of me. Nobody can, and I can't either.
>
> If I tell the truth, you won't believe it. I like to drink. I like parties. I like men. I have been here for four years off and on. I am a prostitute. I have prostituted since a long time. Since a year I have been prostituting with colored men. They think this is the worst, but I tell you I like them better. They treat me with more respect.
>
> I take narcotics—yellow jackets, and there's a strong cough syrup. First it is fun, but then no more. No, it's not yet a habit, so I don't feel very sick when it's taken away.

Sixteen-year-old Dorothy is another one who has "given up," who lives up to what one expects of her, to her own disgust with herself.

Dorothy is the kind of delinquent who fits the stereotype. She seems hard-bitten, looks much older than her age. When Dorothy is seen by a policeman in the streets, he immediately arrests her. It is understood by him that she will make trouble. Dorothy's record is a mile long. Her offenses range from running away to stealing to resisting arrest to prostitution.

Dorothy has no home. She never has known her father. When she was brought to court for the first time at the age of ten, her mother was in the workhouse for drunkenness. The child had witnessed her mother being brutally treated by a man who lived with her. Like many other children, Dorothy went from one institution to another.

There was a short period where she lived with her grandmother who was old and worn out, but who meant something to Dorothy. During that time her behavior improved. But grandmother was poor. One day she was locked out of her apartment, because she failed to pay the rent.

Dorothy was placed somewhere else, and the stealing and running started all over again. In her record, Dorothy is described as being deeply suspicious, showing marked hostility toward authority, with disregard of every social custom and absence of guilt feelings. To some observers she seemed to be satisfied with herself and to have no wish to have any relationship with others.

I met Dorothy when she was in solitary confinement, because she had tried to escape from the institution. She looked unkempt, and was deprived of her clothing. At first she refused to talk. When I offered Dorothy my comb and brush she hesitated, then reached for them with a look in her eye which clearly said, "Now you will snatch them from me. You would not really want *me* to share them with you, would you?" When nothing happened, she began to brush and comb her hair.

Suddenly she began to talk. The words were harsh and full of her anger, but there was hidden sorrow. I wish I could have taken a film instead of the recording. Dorothy constantly kept her head turned away from me, leaning back. She was close to tears. Whenever I looked down on my notes, Dorothy quickly searched my face, obviously trying to find out whether I was shocked. The following are excerpts from her talk with me:

Everything makes me mad. My whole life, the life here. You can't talk to anybody. You can't trust anybody. I have been here off and on for two years. I can't trust anyone. I kind of like my social worker, but I can't trust her or simply nobody. Other girls? No, they too can't be trusted. They tell on you.

Think of it! I will be four to six weeks in a locked room! I have been here already for eleven days. All in all, I have been in solitary for about fifty-two weeks. I get out, and I run away. It's no use. I think all the time, I think and rethink. *I feel terribly lonely. No, I don't talk about it to anyone.* It is no use. I read books, but they don't have very good ones here. Once a day you are allowed to go to the toilet. Otherwise, there is the stinking pot.

I think it's no use to even try. I will always get into trouble. I learned the things here about prostitution, and I will continue. I don't care. I know what I will do with my life: *I will always run away, or I will quit altogether.* I am a prostitute, and I don't think that is so terrible. No, it doesn't bother me. I just don't care. I learned it here, and I make a good living with it. I started out by writing bad checks. Now I prostitute. I do it for money. Money is good. You need money.

The whole thing started when I stole. I stole money from a man. When he wanted to attack me, I pulled a knife. I wouldn't anymore.

I started stealing when I was eight or nine years old. I was scared when they put me in jail, but only at first. Then I thought I would get out, and I wasn't scared anymore.

All I want is to be left alone. If I would get out I would get a job and prostitute on the side. Sure, there are other ways of making money. I would prefer other ways of making money, but where can I earn as much as a prostitute? I couldn't get any other jobs. I can go as a waitress, but a waitress doesn't earn as much as a prostitute.

I don't feel like going back to school. There's no subject that interests me.

No, I have never trusted or loved anybody. I don't know my father. I always had only older friends. I never cared for kids my own age.

What I think of my life as an adult? I would live the same life as I have now. Only I don't want to be here. They just should not catch me.

I am not scared of venereal disease. I can get all the shots. Pregnant? I won't be pregnant. I just won't. If I ever get caught, I'll have an abortion. I know where to get it. I learned that here too. Dangerous? *It makes absolutely no difference to me if I live or die. I don't like this life but there is no other.*

All I want is not to live in poverty. I don't even want for another childhood. I have never thought of the future. I don't think of it. My dream? I want to be rich. I want to have a car and clothes and jewelry. I want to travel. I want a house. I want to be by myself. *I don't want to be dependent,* and people shouldn't ask me questions.

Dorothy will not "change" easily. She is one of the girls who does not even pretend to want to change. Dorothy allows us a glimpse into the abysmal despair of those who see no way out, to whom the normal "way of life" is so foreign that it ceases to make any sense, and yet Dorothy also is a teenager like all the others, who cries inside herself, who wishes she were not so alone, who would live differently if she could see any chance to be "like others." But without hope she proves to herself and others that she really *is* worthless and lives up to her low opinion of herself.

Underneath the stubborn pretense in almost all the girls is a yearning for recognition, support, and "another life."

The eighteen-year-old who fiercely protested that she needed nobody, that she "didn't care what *they* did to her," confided to herself:

Alone with My Thoughts

Today as I sit here in my dark and lonely room,
My heart is full of sorrow and in gloom;
I think of all the wrong I have done,
But as for regrets—I have none.
I'm sorry for those I hurt who love me;
Let their hearts feel compassion and pity me.
If I had the chance to live my life again,
I'd do it the same, knowing I'd lose in the end.
In my heart I know it's wrong living so cheap,
I can't change now, and all I do is cry and weep,
Maybe someday I'll be a different girl;
When I am alone to face this big, big world.
Maybe one day I'll see the light,
And the wrong things will turn to right.
But if that day should never come,
Remember me as "the hurt and lonely one."

7. EMERGING THEORY

*I am a Person like everyone else
yet different in my own right.
I am lonely, surrounded by a
faceless world.
I am a young girl caught in a
deeply changing world.*

We have listened. We have heard pain, anger, hatred, frustration. We have tried to understand without too much of a preconceived theory. We wanted to find out whether the girl in our society is confronted with some specific problems, particular to her as a girl, which may lead to unacceptable behavior. We were not totally satisfied with the theories regarding delinquency brought forward by other thinkers and researchers. Did we find some additional clues to understanding? I surmise that the girls themselves helped us to see some very particular and clear outlines significant for the understanding of those who come into serious conflict with society.

I am aware of the fact that I saw only a limited population and that more and wider research is necessary. On the other hand this was research in depth, and the population represented three major racial groups. It came from rural and city areas in the middle Northwest of the United States—a population which is rather typical for this country and, with some slight variation, of several countries of Western Europe. And information repeated itself significantly in listening to the over two hundred girls questioned and worked with.

What is "theory"? It can be defined in different ways. I like to look at it as an arrangement of findings in a systematic form. Can this be done with the preceding material without violating the infinite variety of human behavior and emotions we have found?

We must try, while warning ourselves against generalizations when we meet any particular girl in reality. It is important to remember that theory is always only a screen which helps to sift ideas, to understand better. It never applies totally and unchangeably to one individual. It allows for many combinations and always for exceptions.

The theory which emerges is by necessity a complex one. It does not see the girl's delinquency as lying exclusively in her personality. It goes beyond a view of an individual wholistic theory which stresses the interaction of physical and psychological forces, though it must take those into account. It does not explain the girl's delinquency out of sociological-cultural circumstances alone, though it does and must include the significance of the human and economic environment.

We have not yet a language which expresses an integration of the whole personality as part of his human relationships and the total culture surrounding it. The limitation of language forces me to present the theory in its significant parts.

The key concepts I found are:

1. The unique dramatic biological onset of puberty in the girl
2. The complex identification process
3. The changing cultural position of women
4. The "faceless" adult authority and the resulting loneliness

I will summarize in an organized form the findings presented in the previous chapters around those key concepts and enlarge on them. I will omit all general knowledge pertaining to adolescence. The framework in which we understand the girl in conflict is the one of adolescence with the characteristics known to exist during this age period. They are known and need no repetition, and most of them apply to boys and girls alike. I will only pull together what is particular to the adolescent girl in our time and what may contribute to what is called delinquent behavior.

1. The Specific Meaning of the Biological Onset of Puberty in the Girl

This onset is different from the one in the boy. It is more marked and resembles injury. It is exceptionally frightening if the girl is not prepared for it. It requires a positive acceptance of regular and recurring bodily changes.

Closely related to this is the biological task of bearing children, which influences the attitude toward sex—in whatever form. It must be significantly different in the girl than in the boy. The *consequence* of the sex act is always present—consciously or unconsciously. It involves the total personality, cannot be separated out, as it may be for the boy. Pregnancy itself changes the total body of the girl and therefore involves the personality. Sex, therefore, has a more pervasive meaning to the girl. Intense romantic connotation—pervasive frigidity, sex as outlet for frustration, sex as a weapon—may be developed.

It is doubtful that sexual acting out is more frequent in girls than in boys—the contrary seems to be true. Yet it is more evident to the public because of the significant meaning it has to the girl herself and because society is generally negative toward it for the girl while tolerant of it for the boy.

2. The Complex Psychological Identification Process

All children, boys and girls alike, pass early through a period of intensive love of the parent of the opposite sex and later learn to identify with the one of their own sex. This process is complicated in the girl by the fact that she must return for feminine identification to the person who nurtured her as a baby. This creates special resistance and explains the frequent conflict with mothers in early adolescence. It may be worked through successfully if both mother and father are giving, protecting, and limiting human beings.

Absence of the father, brutality of the father, competitiveness or weakness or strong domination by the mother make the identification very difficult or impossible.

3. The Changing Cultural Position of Women

This cultural change is deeply significant because it involves the fabric of the family and basic values in relation to the worth of human beings. The following aspects of this change have the greatest impact on the girl's behavior:

(a) *No tradition of vocational training for women,* though hard work for women of low economic background is traditional.

(b) *Stereotyped and low-paying employment for women.* There is no tradition of self-help to improve working conditions because working women themselves look upon employment as temporary. The adolescent working girl sees marriage frequently as "the way out" of undesirable work situations.

(c) *Thwarted ambition,* only partially related to economics. This is the Cloward-Ohlin theory in regard to delinquency of boys. For girls it is directly related to being a *woman.* The exceptional girl can enter various vocations. The average one is still highly confined.

(d) *Little legitimate outlet for aggressive drives.* The ideal image of the girl is still "sugar and spice." The natural adolescent drive for adventure may be satisfied through activities not accepted by society or through provision of it by boys, who have easier access to the tools for it, e.g., cars.

(e) *Increased awareness and resentment of the "double standard."* This resentment, a result of the stress on supposed equality of the sexes, is transferred to any other "double standard," especially to inequality regarding race.

4.   The Faceless Adult Authority and the Resulting Loneliness

The preceding three points apply to all adolescent girls. They may lead to delinquency under special conditions, as described in the preceding chapters and mentioned shortly under each point. This fourth concept applies exclusively to the girls who have come into conflict with society. Authority at home, in school, and in all other significant parts of their lives (recreation and law enforcement, for instance) is not experienced as *people,* but only strangers who make demands. Authority is not seen as a protector, as a loving force, even as a human being one knows. It is encountered as an enemy force one must duck, circumvent, or fight. Because distrust grows so strongly, it invades even relationships to contemporaries.

Friendship becomes unknown. The ways out of total and frightening isolation are the joining of the crowd or engaging in romantic relationships.

The resulting behavior usually leads to rejection by the community, general experience of having no recognized success (School!), increasingly low self-image, and more behavior which increases the feeling of worthlessness. The vicious cycle continues.

I will try to present the theory I have described in a scheme. I do hope that some day I will be able to continue and refine the research, and that others will also contribute to it.

Scheme of a Theory Pertaining to the Adolescent Girl in Conflict

I. *Specific and significant aspects of adolescence in all girls*

Violent biological onset of puberty
Pervasiveness of sexual task
Complex identification process
Present changing culture includes:
　　Limited vocational choice
　　Little tradition of learning and preparation for employment
　　Little outlet for aggressive drives
　　Double standard

II. *Related conditions which may lead to delinquency*

No preparation for biological onset of puberty
$$\downarrow \quad \text{(produces)}$$
　　Fear—resentment—experimentation

No preparation for pervasiveness of sexual task or poor preparation
$$\downarrow \quad \text{(produces)}$$
　　Fear—disgust—experimentation with own or other sex

Identification process made impossible by brutal or absent father, competitive or weak mother
$$\downarrow \quad \text{(produces)}$$
Rejection of femininity

Limited vocational choice increased by low economic status, little stimulation
$$\downarrow \quad \text{(produces)}$$
　　Resentment of work—"being supported" as way out

Little tradition of learning and preparation for employment
$$\downarrow \quad \text{(produces)}$$
　　School failure and same as above

Highly thwarted aggressive drive

$\qquad$ ↓ (produces)

    Stealing—sex adventure—sometimes physical abuse of other people

Double standard

$\qquad$ ↓ (produces)

    Resentment—individual revenge and violation of standards—no joining of a *movement*

III. *General picture*

    Excessive loneliness
    Low self-image
    Estrangement from adult society
    Incapacity for friendship with contemporaries

$\qquad$ ↓ (produces)

    Losing oneself in the crowd

    Search for romantic involvement

$\qquad$ ↓ (produces)

    Rejection by society

$\qquad$ ↓ (produces)

    More delinquent behavior or self-destruction

8. WE ARE RESPONSIBLE

*I think we harden somewhat in
our hearts,
And look, perhaps, too close on
one another
Searching too swiftly for a neigh-
bor's fault
In the cold Winters when the
dark comes soon,
For Thou art sun and light as
well, my God.*[1]

No difficulty confronting society can ever be totally erased.
The biggest advancements in medical knowledge have not yet prevented the occurrence of illness. But improvements can be made;
existing knowledge can and must be used. The "We" in the title
of this chapter was carefully chosen. It includes all of us: the girls
themselves and also every member of the communities around
them. Changes of attitude, of behavior, of thinking, or feeling
must come in the last instance from the person himself; there is
no way out of this. Yet help is necessary to everyone at some time
in his life. Youth, especially, needs help from the adult world.
Adults have the difficult responsibility of raising the young to be
part of an orderly world, a lawful world, a world in which each
individual can develop his capacities. He must also accept the
limitations which come through the interdependence of people and
his responsibility for others. At the same time, adults must also
accept the fact that each generation must find its way, its own
forms of living together. Robert Frost wrote so beautifully,

---

[1] Stephen Vincent Benét, *Western Star* (New York: Holt, Rinehart & Winston, Inc., 1943), p. 171. Copyright 1943 by Rosemary Carr Benét. Reprinted by
permission of Brandt & Brandt.

I think that young people have insight. They have a flash here and a flash there. It's like the stars coming out in the early evening. They have flashes of light. They have that sort of thing which belongs to youth. It is later in the dark of life that you see forms, constellations.[2]

Even though the "flashes of light" youth perceives and the actions based on them are not always comfortable to the adult world, if they do not harm others directly or indirectly, they should be accepted. Harmfulness is not easily assessed. Mistakes in two opposite directions—too much restriction or too much leniency— can easily be made. They can be diminished by a determined effort on the part of those who work with youth to use available knowledge and not be swayed by emotions. To make this possible, to help "the Girl in Conflict," we need first of all a community climate which says *yes* to youth—neither by idolizing it nor by fearing it, but by accepting youth as a significant partner with rights and responsibilities, with opportunities for development and genuine participation in the making of society—a never-ending task. Such an attitude will contribute to a growing sense of cooperation between the generations. Honesty in admitting the shortcomings, injustices, and mistakes, with an encouragement to look for improvement are the prerequisite of a healthy community climate.

This, then, is the base on which we may build more specific suggestions to help the adolescent girl in conflict. We know that, in general, the attitude of society is especially harsh toward the delinquent girl. It is one of disinterest or fear or moral indignation. The problem of communication between the generations is accentuated and services to girls are especially poor, because most of the girls act out sexually and this behavior touches the core of every human personality. Many adults carry conflicts, guilt, repressed wishes, and confusion with them in this area. These uncertainties are transmitted to the girls, leaving them as badly confused as the adult—sometimes defiant, sometimes withdrawn. We see that girls, especially those from economically and socially deprived backgrounds, have had appallingly little sex information, and much of what they had was false. Most girls find themselves confused because of the still prevailing double standard for boys and girls, and because of conflicting precepts which pronounce sex as healthy and good on the one hand and as base and sinful on the other. Quite clearly there is a need in this area for a preventive program: availability of sex education for adults and youngsters, with a clear,

[2] Quoted by Michael Drury, "Robert Frost," *McCall's Magazine*, LXXXVII: 7 (April 1960), 148.

simple, and frank explanation of biological facts and an opportunity for questions and discussion of attitudes. Skilled discussion leaders who can use simple language and elicit participation are essential in such programs. In many families, parents are incapable of discussing these subjects because they are frightened themselves or do not know how to express themselves. Relationships between the girls and their parents often make such communication impossible, usually at a time when it is most needed. If they could attend such meetings together, more than sex information may be gained. They may learn to talk to each other about significant concerns. Such education may be possible in some schools, but many schools, unfortunately, have large classes which do not lend themselves easily to the free interchange of ideas on such an emotionally charged subject, and teachers are not always trained to handle it. Also, the delinquent girl is often the one who absents herself from classes and therefore would not get the advantage of sex information in the classroom.

Community centers, youth-serving agencies, churches, recreational and social agencies should take responsibility for reaching every girl who comes within their purview and for holding sex discussions in small groups—at times including parents—conducted by their most skilled, sensitive, and knowledgeable personnel. Such sessions should be held even before the onset of puberty, and need to be repeated on different levels at later developmental stages. These discussions should not be used to frighten the girls or to warn them of "consequences." They should be designed to help them to accept their femininity with a clear knowledge and a healthy positive sense of responsibility.

Sex education for boys and adults should be directed especially toward erasing the "double standard." The girls are aware of—and deeply resentful of—the fact that premarital sex relations are still considered a matter of pride to many boys and their elders, and that they may boast about them. The double standard is almost as old as humanity, but in this age when women live in a society which claims to consider men and women of equal worth, adolescent girls rebel more intensely against this form of hypocrisy. Change of societal attitudes will come through a new education of boys and young men toward acceptance of their share of responsibility, not only for the child who might be born, but also for the dignity and happiness of the sex partner. The acceptance of the double standard as something inevitable can no longer be tolerated.

The problem of prostitution is definitely not a question of female delinquency alone. As a social problem it includes economic deprivation and the attitude of men. As a personal problem it lies in the area of emotional disturbance and cannot be significantly improved through prohibitive ordinances.

Many other existing services for girls need revaluation and radical change. The following seem most important:

1. There Should Be a New Approach to Services for Unmarried Mothers

It has become obvious that old theories regarding unmarried mothers as "neurotic" or as "unconsciously hostile," etc., must be discarded.

Sex relations—if based on love—are considered permissible by many young people who represent a wide range of emotional maturity and intelligence. Pregnancies out of wedlock occur in girls of this wide range of intelligence, knowledge, and maturity and in all socio-economic levels of the population.

A gynecologist, who sees predominantly middle-class girls and women of a student population, observed that girls today are less desperate about an unwed pregnancy than they were two decades ago. She no longer encounters a large number of suicides or suicide attempts because of pregnancy. Yet she found girls very disturbed because of the violation of a basic female need, the wish to be a mother. Certainly there are girls and women who do not want the child they carry, and there are many who are strongly ambivalent about it. Yet there seems to be an increasing number who want to keep their child. Usually they are discouraged from doing this. There have been—and still are—societies which punish the unmarried mother by forcing her to keep her child, even under distressing and humiliating conditions. Our society, under the guise of a free decision, uses a subtle form of pressure in the opposite direction. The unmarried mother is made to feel that she is totally selfish if she keeps her child. This pressure comes from both family members and professional people. Even if the social worker tries to help the girl to make her own decision, the provisions made for helping unmarried mothers raise their children with dignity are practically nil. Very few day-care services for working mothers exist. Not only are grants for mothers to stay home small, but those who receive them are too often exposed to community scorn. What kind of value system do we transmit to the unmarried mother?

It is a strange contradiction that, while we hope to educate girls for responsibility, we act—not always, but frequently—as if the child they are carrying is a tumor which must be forgotten as soon as it is "removed."

It is also paradoxical that, while we are trying to educate young people to be truthful, we provide an elaborate network of lies and hiding places during the pregnancy, usually to save the "good reputation" of the family. To avoid any misunderstanding: such places of refuge are needed today, should exist, and unmarried mothers should not hesitate to use them. Yet the need for their existence indicts the basic hypocrisy of our total society.

It is a strange contradiction that a society which knows about the need of pregnant women to be protected, to have support before and after the birth of a child, almost completely disregards this knowledge when a delinquent girl is in this situation. Homes for non-delinquent unmarried mothers provide some comfort and protection. Delinquency institutions frequently give only physical care to the pregnant girl. Many exclude her specifically from the comforting presence of others. In some such institutions, the pregnant delinquent girl is segregated from her companions. Delivery of the baby is in a bleak hospital room with no comforting adult present. One of the young girls I saw was in hysterical terror when she anticipated "her time" and realized that she had to go through this without any support.

After the birth of a child, girls are returned to the institution and often admonished not to speak to others about their experience. There is total disregard of post-partem depression. A fifteen-year-old began to sob furiously when I started to interview her, crying that she did not understand what had happened to her, that she felt like killing herself. This girl had delivered a baby two days before, had been separated from her child, and was supposed to re-enter immediately the routine of the delinquency institution. Nobody was concerned or had prepared her for a possible depression.

Based on these preceding observations, some tangible suggestions for services to unmarried mothers can be made:

(a) Services to delinquent pregnant girls should include provisions for physical and emotional support necessary to the well-being of any woman before, during, and after childbirth. This is not "mollycoddling." Such treatment does not create irresponsibility. On the contrary, it may make the girl feel that she is a woman with responsibility for a new life. A sense of responsibility is defeated if the girl feels that only her child is considered a worthy person, but not she herself.

(b) Provisions should be made for adequate and loving care of young children of working mothers with no differentiation between children born legitimately and those born out of wedlock.

(c) Better support is needed for those mothers who want to stay home and raise their children. There should be a core of volunteer or paid child-care experts, women who are a combination of public health nurse and social worker who visit mothers of *all* newborn babies to see whether they need help. Such service is available, in some countries, to everyone, regardless of economic need, to avoid any stigma of "charity" or implication of "inadequacy." These women could then give more intensive and long-range help to the girls who must carry alone the burden of raising a child. The young mothers usually know little physically, mentally, or emotionally about child rearing. Because these young women themselves need so much support, the child-care visitor should come not as an investigator, but as a friend. She should have the skill to enter quickly into the lives of the mother, children, and neighborhood. Her helping skill should include the organizing of informal neighborhood groups of women who can share their concerns, and continue as self-help groups.

2. There Should Be a Revaluation of the Status of Women

Because of the changing status of women, a fresh look must be taken at the employment opportunities, salaries, wages, and vocational education for girls. Employment and marriage should be seen as equally important life tasks of girls, so that they learn to prepare themselves realistically for both. This will help to begin a tradition of schooling for the girl, raise wages, and give her incentive to lawful employment. It is not sufficient to ask for "equal pay for equal work." Typical women's work needs to be upgraded, even if no men are at present employed in those occupations. The job of the waitress demands as much physical effort as the work of a bricklayer, yet at present, wages of the two cannot be compared. A cleaning woman works as hard as a window cleaner, but again her wage is far below that of her male counterpart.

Employment preparation for the girl should place her alongside
the boy, and should include occupations which have not been
traditionally open to women. Today girls are being trained for
skilled labor in industry and in other technical occupations, in
communication skills, or in driving trucks. This should be enlarged.
Opportunities for such training should be made available in delinquency institutions. Too many girls' training schools restrict their
training to household service and beauty care. Both are perfectly
legitimate, necessary, and, for some girls, attractive occupations,
but not all girls find satisfaction from them. Furthermore, household work has always been notoriously underpaid. An upgrading
of these more traditional "feminine" positions through increased
monetary compensation and better, more independent working ar-
rangements may make this work more attractive and acceptable to
girls with a thirst for independence and self-sufficiency. The same
applies to service positions which can be performed under supervision. Institutions for the retarded, nursing homes for the aged,
and mental hospitals are desperately understaffed. Teenagers bring
a fresh life into those places and make them more cheerful. If they
get some help, teenagers have an amazing stamina in working with
difficult and tedious people. Aside from recruiting teenagers as
volunteers for such work, there should be a number of paying
positions for young girls in the helping services.

There is also the whole area of vocations which allow some
satisfaction of the young person's thirst for adventure. There should
be an effort to open more opportunities for girls in fields such as
aviation, soil conservation, forestry, and the performing arts. These
fields are still too closed against girls and especially against those
who have shown rebellious behavior. A college girl who had made
excellent grades confided that her ambition had been to become a
forester. She had been told that this was no choice for a woman.
Adequate pay and training for a large variety of jobs, vocations,
and professions will help the rebellious and maverick girl to feel
better accepted, and give her positive instead of destructive outlets
for her energies.

Such opportunities and beginning preparation for interesting,
useful employment should be a major task for communities and
delinquency institutions, instead of the deadly "do-nothing" or
"make-do" filling of time existing today. Individualized vocational
counseling with a realistic, yet unstereotyped, search for employment and schooling is as necessary as other rehabilitative work.
Some helping efforts should be directed toward the girl's look into
her past as she works through the underlying conflicts. But this

is only one part of therapy. Hope must be added and a look into a different and realistically possible future.

3. A Hard Look at and Change in Youth Services

It is not surprising that a majority of offenses for which girls appear before juvenile court include running away from home, truancy, drinking, and sex experiences. One significant reason, among others, is the dull, uninspired, and often conflict-ridden life they lead at home and in school. Also, routes for the normal outlet of teenage thirst for adventure, for excitement, and for significant group relations and action are practically non-existent. Present youth-serving organizations started in the early part of the twentieth century. Their organization filled the given needs at that particular time. In spite of great cultural change they have kept this organization. Most of them are one-sex organizations, or at least are so designated.[3] They are frequently bound to a particular denomination or religious faith. Some have a rigidly outlined program with a hierarchy of offices. All those qualities may still appeal to youth who come from orderly homes, who are capable of living in such a structure, or who have developed sufficient self-confidence and leadership skill to effect changes within it.

It is known that clubs are predominantly a middle-class phenomenon and have an important role to play. Fewer people in the lower economic strata belong to such groups. Children from this background do not see their elders participating in club activities. Again, as pointed out earlier, the girl in this population is especially incapable of entering highly structured entities, cannot make friends on her own. She resents anything that "smells" like reform ("character building"). Like all girls today, she is used to free interaction with boys and she wants to be with them. Her drives are strong and diffused. She needs excitement, not tame (and to her, often "childish") activities.

New coed youth services are needed with especially knowledgeable, gifted, imaginative group workers in charge. Activities should include the new world with its excitement, but also allow for the

[3] The most prominent youth organizations are Boy Scouts, Girl Scouts, Camp Fire Girls, the Y's, Boys Clubs, religious youth organizations. The author is aware of the fact that many of them conduct coed activities, and that the Hebrew Y's are coeducational. Settlement and neighborhood houses offer coed activities.

quiet intimate discussions so necessary to teenage girls. The girls are surrounded by travel posters and the tales of privileged youth who go across the ocean. Most of them can see other parts even of their own country only when they take a ride in a stolen car. Wilderness trips for probationers have proved themselves far more effective than endless discussions across the desk. A probation department has started weekend programs for boys at the local airport. They learn about ground activities and are occasionally taken on short flights. There is no reason why something like this should not also be available for girls.

New youth services should take into account the conditions under which many of the girls grow up. The term "culture of poverty" has become fashionable, yet I hesitate using it, because it may imply a stereotype and an assumption that poor people have completely differing values and mores from the surrounding society. Poor people are not only individually different, but there are many subgroups and differing attitudes among them. And certainly, the deprived youngster lives in the same society as all the other youngsters, often goes to the same school, sees the same movies, eats some of the same food. Their hopes and aspirations are similar. Yet there *is* a difference compared with their contemporaries from a middle-class background. The fulfillment of dreams is not only further removed, but often seems unreachable. Their homes provide little stimulation for the mind. There are no books, no discussions on current events, no explanation of the problems or questions brought up in school. Youth workers, therefore, need to know more than adolescent psychology or theories about differing value systems. They should experience the environment in which the girls with whom they work live.

Informal home visits (the age-old method of the settlement houses) are indispensable. Youth workers who do not come from the same background as the girls should spend evenings with those families and live through the noise, the fighting, and the frustration. They should learn about the generosity of poverty which may allow a stranger to sleep in an already overcrowded room, because he has no other place to stay. There is no privacy and maybe it is not valued highly. They may encounter the fierce loyalty among people who feel themselves "outsiders." Thus they may learn to understand that there is a "united front" against authority, though at home there are quarrels and dissent. A girl may say that she hates her mother (and mean it), but she will deny it and hate the outsider who tries to remove her from her mother. Such insights will help the youth worker to work more effectively with the girl and the whole family; they will also make him a most valuable partner of the schools who need and want to adapt their curriculum to the needs of deprived youngsters. They will become serious partners in the total field of mental health—in prevention as well as treatment. The intense interaction with the family of the girls in their own home environment or with the girls alone or in groups in their own neighborhood should have two other salutary consequences:

(a) The powerful adult world of authority and respectability which is at present "anonymous" to most of the girls will gain an identity. By eating together, laughing together, sitting together in a crowded room, the youth worker and the girls will get to know each other. And the youth worker may make a conscious part of the program some social visiting with teachers, judges, business leaders. Authority becomes *persons, people* whom one may trust.

(b) Such interaction may lead to action by the girls themselves for improvement of their situation, not only individually, but as part of a community. With a sense of being accepted and wanted as a participant in community development comes a sense of dignity and responsibility.

The traditional pattern of community organization has been the establishment of committees of citizens on the top of the community power structure to work on behalf of those who need help. Yet most significant changes in services have occurred through self-help groups. Those who participated in them gained indirectly also something for themselves, especially self-esteem. The hidden strength of our more deprived youth, and especially the girl, is virtually untapped. It would be tragic if it were to be misused by demagogues against a democratic society or if it stays—as today—confined to delinquent acts. The development of a much larger number of more competent and compassionate youth workers—teachers and social group workers—who can combine concern for the individual girl with concern for the whole community and have the skill to help her to involve herself, becomes urgent.

4. Reshaping of Delinquency Services According to Present-Day Knowledge

All professions and services develop historically. They start to fulfill a need at a given time—sometimes perceived by a few, sometimes by many. In the course of time there is usually a cultural lag between what the service ought to be and what it is. This lag is very strong in correctional services, probably because there is no self-interest group speaking for them. The lag is especially great in delinquency services for girls. If the keys to the understanding of the girl in conflict are individual differences, extreme loneliness in a faceless world, and the cultural position of girls, then preventative and treatment services should relate to these. Many of the general community services discussed in the three preceding suggestions, if well established and carried through, would make far fewer delinquency services necessary. Yet even these services cannot completely eliminate the need for delinquency services. The girls who come under those services are the ones who are in greatest need and who have the most severe problems. The community expects of them a change in behavior, but such changes are rarely accomplished or are of short duration when there is not an inner motivation toward such change and an environment which offers reasonable opportunities for beginning and continuing acceptable behavior. Motivation grows out of relationship with other human beings; trust develops a wish to live up to expectations. It is logical that the delinquent girl needs adults who can help her develop trust and who can give her support, who can help her develop confidence in herself so that she feels able and strong enough to live up to standards. Because this development takes time, *continuous* relationships with an understanding adult are essential. The traditional design of movement from probation to institution to parole seldom, if ever, permits such continued relationships. No one person stays with the girl. This increases her distrust, her loneliness, and her conception of an "anonymous" world of authority. In addition to this, almost all those people—with the exception of the police and the judge—are women. There is, then, practically no opportunity to establish a positive picture of men—a necessity for the girl who had either no father or a brutal one.

The majority of social workers dealing with delinquent girls are young college women with little professional training in social work. They usually have been more protected from encounters with the seamier side of life than their male counterparts. The gulf between these young women and the girls with whom they work is enormous. The delinquent girls do not feel that they can talk freely with their social workers. The young women themselves who come to this kind of work with idealistic but often unrealistic expectations soon experience disillusionment and feel insecure, frightened, and threatened. They frequently change from an ardent, well-meaning but totally unrealistic wish to "save" or help these girls to hard-bitten, angry distrust of them. Expressions such as "The girl just gives me a snow job" or "The girl is fronting" are symbols of the feelings of those disillusioned young women. This makes it impossible for them to accept the girl with her potential. This attitude is very human. Yet professional work demands self-discipline, rigorous self-confrontation in spite of personal disappointment or hurt, if it is to continue to be helpful.

The same applies to cottage personnel who start with a genuine wish to help and who shower their maternal feelings on those "poor kids." Unprepared for the hostility and distrust of the girls, they begin to retaliate. They, too, usually come from backgrounds which were comfortable and stable. To them people who are different often have to be suspected as "bad." Their disillusionment turns into disgust and fear. They often had good intentions. They needed support too. Fearful people are most dangerous, they hit out, they torture. If they are in power, they are especially damaging.

All delinquency services need to be re-examined. There is a need for a continuum of services to youth in trouble while they live in their own home, to substitute services by placement in foster homes, group homes, or small institutions.

All delinquency services, especially institutions, need more and better personnel.

Program in delinquency institutions should avoid practices which only humiliate and decrease self-respect, and thus only intensify hostile attitudes toward society.

All delinquency institutions need more imaginative programs of schooling, informal education, and special treatment, which should permeate the total living situation. This is not the place to go into detail on all these points. I will name those needs specifically pertinent to treatment of the delinquent adolescent girl:

(a) Staff selection and training must include insight into the professional's own feelings regarding sex and the position of women in our society. Because of the particular nature of the girl's delinquency, people working with girls need to be familiar with the wide variety of human emotions and must be able to accept twisted and impoverished lives, using resources from their own rich and healthy private lives to aid in their understanding. They need to combine rigorous professional self-discipline with the capacity to convey warmth.

(b) Professional staff should include both men and women and, if possible, people from different races and strata of the population so that the image of the harshly divided world—as perceived by the girls—begins to disappear.

(c) Schooling and vocational guidance should take into account and accept the change in women's position and the particular problems girls face on the labor market.

(d) Delinquency institutions for girls should make special room for the visual arts, drama, and writing. Creative work presents a legitimate outlet for emotions, including aggression, for women. They fit into the girl's need for adornment and expression. They may even become channels for future employment.

(e) All delinquency services for girls must understand the vital significance the youngsters have for each other. Many years ago Kenneth Wollan wrote:

> I would hazard the judgment that during the next 25 years the most important remedial work in institutions will be done through group therapy and the careful planning of group experience.[4]

This should be so, but it is not yet sufficiently carried through. Some forms of group work or group therapy have been modeled too much after the "desk" approach, with a simple question and answer game. Good group work focuses on interaction of the group members in addition to problems of each individual, on mutual help, the working through of conflict, the use of an informal situation without misusing it. The group approach is indispensable in the institution. Groups of parolees are just as necessary on the "outside" to help the girls over their feeling of isolation, their need for mutual support, their need to discuss the temptations in every day life and to continue the learning of friendship.

(f) Volunteer services given by adults and other young people should become a vital part of work with delinquent girls. The Big

[4] Kenneth I. Wollan, "The Influence of Psychiatry on the Institutional Care of Delinquents" (Round Table, Psychiatry and Delinquency, 1948; William Healy, M.D., Chairman) *American Journal of Orthopsychiatry*, XIX: 2 (April 1949), 336.

Sister idea should enter the delinquency field. Women who are willing to become friends and confidantes of the delinquent girl must not expect "sugar and spice." They must be willing to continue their relationship, even when they are disappointed over and over again. Many of the girls have never experienced the basic emotional nourishment of a child—unconditional love. They must experience this before they can learn to make themselves worthy of trust.

Young people should become a consciously used resource to help the delinquent girl. At present, she feels unaccepted by the "good" girls. Parents warn their daughters against a girl who is known to have been in a delinquency institution. This is understandable, but how will the girl ever move out of her unhappy isolation? Every school and every youth organization should be able to draw from a pool of reliable young volunteers ready to make friends with a returnee from an institution and to draw her into the circle of other youngsters. There should be no condescension, just one youngster approaching another.

It is *we,* the community, who must reach out, even though in the last resort, it is each person himself who must learn to conduct his life. No "pill" can be given to make him do something. The raised finger, the punishment, the admonishment all come from the outside and are rarely lasting, if at all successful. In the end, real change must come from the girl herself. But she cannot achieve change by herself. The glass wall separating her from others allows her only to see them, but not to feel them. In this cold separation she feels lost and confused. Once more I let one of them speak of this herself:

I am a juvenile—a juvenile delinquent
And I hate this label.
Even if the words had no meaning, they sound hard and condemning
And say that I am bad.
Yet I am not really so different from the girls who seem to me
Smug in their goodness.

I often think that no one cares about how I feel.
I wish they would try to understand me as they claim they want to;
I wish they would listen to what I have to say and
Not think of what they want to say to me.

People are always claiming that they want to help me—
My parents, teachers, social workers—
All tell me this, but I wonder what they mean by help.

Is it to make me over to be like them?
This is not for me.

At times I feel all hollow inside as though I were afraid—
Of what I'm not really sure.
However, this feeling leaves me when I get high.
When I take pills, I feel great;
Nothing is too difficult for me to do—
I think better, I'm really sharp.

I have no problems so I do not worry—
It's great to be high!
They told me at the hospital that I must stop
Because next time I might not be so lucky.
But how can I promise for tomorrow?

I remember when I started dating in junior high
My mother was all for it.
She made a big thing of it because I was popular
And had lots of boys coming around.
When I told her I was going to have a baby,
She said I was boy crazy and she was ashamed of me.
But she had it all wrong.
Many times I had the feeling that I didn't even like boys;
I know I never thought of getting married.

I feel that it is wrong to give away your baby
And so I kept mine.
I may not be a good mother
But at least I kept my baby—
Which I think is a point in my favor.
The baby is cute and I suppose I love her
But I do not want her to tie me down too much.
She has made no difference in the way my friends feel about me.
When they come over, they play with her
And even bring her toys.
But at times we all try to forget that she is around.

Another thing—I not only need an education,
I really want to learn.
School does not believe me when I say this
Because I stay home so frequently
And often do not do the work assigned.
I know that I must change if I am ever to get my diploma
But it is hard for me to be just a student
And follow rules, rules, rules.

I really don't belong in school—
But I need my diploma.
I'm not happy living at home—
But I can't move out with a baby.
I'd like to find a good job—
But I have no training.
I get that hollow feeling and then I wonder
Where do I go from here? [5]

She and all the others need help, and they want it. They do not need degradation which we have too frequently offered them. Degradation breeds hatred and hatred breeds brutality as we have seen in the horrible history of the Nazis and as we experience every day when we deny respect to other human beings.

Help does not come to the girl in conflict through sentimentality. It comes from a realistic understanding of her behavior. It comes from the use of knowledge and insight into the complex makings of a human being. When we have tried to understand, trust may follow, and with it a sense of self-respect for herself. Slowly, sometimes painfully, a bridge between the I and You begins to be built, the glass wall shattered and finally removed.

In a large and confusing world mutual help and friendship are the indispensable base for individual and societal health. Community attitudes must make those possible. Kahlil Gibran reminds us of the interrelatedness of all mankind and how the "good" and "bad" lie side by side in all of us:

> Oftentimes have I heard you speak of one who commits a wrong as though he were not one of you, but a stranger unto you and an intruder upon your world. But I say that even as the holy and the righteous cannot rise beyond the highest which is in each one of you, so the wicked and the weak cannot fall lower than the lowest which is in you also. And as a single leaf turns not yellow but with the silent knowledge of the whole tree, so the wrong-doer cannot do wrong without the hidden will of you all. [6]

When the girls begin to feel that they are part of us, many will begin to change. It would be unrealistic to expect that every single one can be helped to do this. We have not achieved cure or alleviation of even known illnesses in every individual. We can only

[5] Notes taken by school social worker Margaret Erickson.
[6] Kahlil Gibran, *The Prophet* (New York: Alfred A. Knopf, 1951), p. 40. Reprinted by permission of the publisher.

assume that the use of knowledge and practice based on it will be powerful agents in the restoration of a larger number of them and that prevention can be more effective.

The last word should go to one of the girls. Ruth had come to the group work sessions shortly after a suicide attempt, and she had come reluctantly. After some meetings, in halting words, she said about her group experience:

> . . . every time I get more out of this group and I feel more like . . . more like everybody else. I've started to think that, maybe, I am not the worst person in the world. . . . You're not alone.

Now there was hope and a new beginning.

APPENDIX

The reader may be interested in "listening" in on some parts of the group discussions. They show the intensity of feelings, the need to "spill" as well as to think through.

The first one is the fifth session with the same group of older adolescents presented on pages 98-100. They were in a closed institution, a women's reformatory.

Dora escaped from the Reformatory shortly after her friend Peggie had escaped. She had been placed in solitary confinement following her apprehension. The superintendent later granted permission for her to continue to attend the group meetings. This was the first session at which she was present following her escape.

During the first part of the meeting, Dora sat next to Rita, and the two constantly exchanged glances with one another. Rita entered into the group discussion, but Dora had nothing to say.

Rita began to talk softly to her and tried to pull her into the conversation, but she was still quite reticent. The group worker wondered what she had to say. Rita turned the discussion to her:

Rita (to Dora). How do you feel about it? How do you feel about running? Are you sorry?

Dora. No, I am *not* sorry I ran. As I told the group worker, I'm sorry I got caught, but I am not sorry I ran.

[Dora was sharply attacked, especially for having taken a knife with her. The girls tried to force her into admitting that she was "too cowardly" to use a knife. They wanted to show her that she had only tried to imitate Peggie. This showed Dora that the girls saw through her "tough front," but the group worker feared that they were driving her too much into the defensive. She raised the question of whether they wanted her to use the knife. This brought about intensive discussion.]

Rita. How much longer did you have? How much longer did you have before going to the Parole Board?

Dora. To November.

Rita. Now when you go in November, you might get ten more months!

Bertha. You know where you're going to have to live?

Dora. At the high security cottage.

Rita. You're not going to play around with them anymore, and they won't play around with you anymore. You are kicking yourself in the teeth, Dora. This girl right here (*she pointed to Lisa*) . . . You sat there and told her a dirty lie the night before you ran!

Dora. Who? What?

Lisa. . . . that you were happy they had given you leniency. And what did you tell Bertha and Rita on the way home from court? That you felt like telling the Judge to kiss your ass. . . .

Dora. Well, he made me so mad!

Rita. He made *you* mad?

Lisa (*shouting*). You should have thanked that man, Dora. Why don't you stop and think? You've got brains. . . . I've heard you talk better sense than anyone in this damned place. You're not hurting anybody but yourself, Dora, and you're just making a hell on earth for yourself. And you can just sit there and smirk and think it is God-damned funny. Well, *I* don't think it's funny.

Rita (*pointing to Lisa*). That girl cares about you! That girl *really* cares about you, Dora! What's wrong with you?

Dora. I don't know what's wrong with me, Rita.

Group worker. You can speak up. You will make the girls very unhappy if you don't, because they really care.

Rita. You can't turn friendship on and off, but you sure can turn your words on and off.

Group worker. Shall I say it for you? You know, when the girls get angry, they also show how much they care. And I don't think you were just giving me a "snow job" when we talked earlier today, and you said you felt badly.

Dora. No, I did not.

(*Lisa started to cry and left the room.*)

Rita. That girl really cares.

Group worker. Lisa did not shout because she is mad at you, Dora. She is crying *for* you. . . .

Rita. Ask somebody what's wrong. Ask somebody for help. Find out. 'Cause there's gotta be something wrong. Find out what it is. Find out what it is before you really get hurt.

(*Lisa returned to the room.*)

Group worker (turning to Lisa). While you were gone, I think Dora understood that you care.

Lisa (crying). I am going to tell you something else. That night, Dora, when you took off, Amy heard you hit the ground. Mrs. Adams came out into the hall, and she was bawling, and she came into my room to see if I was all right. It was obvious in that damned cottage that I thought a lot of you. And not in any God-damned queer way, either, Dora. And you are just hurting yourself, Dora. You are not hurting anybody else. Just think of all the time you are going to add to yourself, Dora. Do you want to be locked up all your life? My God, Dora, stop and do something now before it is too late. There's a lot of people around here, Dora, that were beginning to get a little bit of faith in you. I sat over there and cried and cried after you left, Dora. If you would only have gone and talked it over with somebody! That's the same thing Miss Scott said to me last Saturday. I had different things building up in me until I felt pretty God-damned mean, until I felt like hitting out at everybody and anybody, and she sat in her office and said to me . . . she said, "This thing about Dora worries you?" And I said, yes. And things like that build up in me, and I'm not used to that anymore.

Bertha. Miss Brighthart talked to me the other day. She asked me what could be done for you. She asked me if I thought marriage would help you.

Rita. Marriage won't help. In order to be helped, Dora, you've got to want to help yourself first.

Lisa. It is just like me, Dora. I've got a lot of problems that I have never told anybody on this earth about. I figured it was just things I had to work out by myself. Some of them I will still never ever reveal to anybody, because they have hurt too deep. But still I can sit down with a book—a psychology book. A lot of it is way over my head, and I will never probably understand it, but when I can understand. . . . But when you come up here, Dora, and sit smirking around like you're the biggest thing around here . . . That hurts. And I am not the only one that thinks a lot of you, Dora. Just like I told you before, underneath that big damned front you put on, you want to be just like other people, Dora; you don't want to be a big, bad thing, and you can be helped if you want to be. It's not too late. You're younger than I am. And you can make this place do something good for you, if you want to. Look at me: I sit over there all the time, sometimes until eleven or twelve o'clock at night, so I can figure out what's wrong with me. And sure, I can help other people too, but I've got to help myself. It's just like I told Miss Scott: other people can give me pointers and say, "Well, maybe it's this or maybe it's that," but I am the only one that can determine what it is that's making me do the things I do. And if you probe hard enough, and if you want to be honest enough with yourself, Dora, you can get to the bottom of it. Now, look! Just think what a name you've made for yourself! When you get out of that cell, Dora, it's not going to be very damned easy, because there are not going to be very many people that are going to give you a chance. And it's going to be some of them trashy, God-damned girls that are going to try and get you into something else. And the officers are going to watch you all the time, Dora, and it is going to get you down. I know it is!

Rita. I hate to see her go back to the security cottage.

Lisa. Yah, but how can you expect anybody to trust her to go any place else? You can't, but Dora has asked for it. It's a cruel thing to say, but she's going to get just what she asked for.

Group worker (to Dora). Why don't you tell the girls how you feel?

Dora. I don't know.

Group worker. You have a lot of feelings about this. Why don't you speak up?

Dora. I don't know what to say. I really don't. . . . Mrs. Konopka, there are so many things I would like to say, but I just can't.

Bertha. Has Rose gotten you into trouble?

Dora. Who?

Bertha. Rose.

Dora. No.

Bertha. Is she your friend? Has Rita gotten you into trouble? Is she your friend? And you think Peggie is really and truly your friend? What kind of a friend is that who is going to get you into as much trouble as you've gotten into?

Dora. Peggie hasn't got me into nothing.

Bertha. If it weren't for Peggie, you wouldn't be sitting here today.

Dora. I couldn't say that.

Rita. No, Dora first ran before Peggie did.

Group worker. Let's go back for a minute to Dora. Let's really help Dora at this moment. (*Turning to Dora*) One thing that struck me when I talked with you alone was that you said there was nobody who really cared for you.

Rita. People that care for her aren't the people she wants.

Group worker. It is a hard thing to begin to trust. But, Dora, listen to that discussion—do you think people get *that* upset if they don't care?

Lisa. You know what she's doing? The same thing I used to do! I didn't think my family cared for me, or that anybody on the outside cared for me. I wanted to hurt them, but instead of hurting them, I hurt myself. I took it all out on me. But right now is the time for her to change. I mean, something's got to give.

Group worker. Dora, can you listen to that, not just with your ear! Try to feel it. Or is that too hard? Do you believe them at all?

Dora. Sure I believe them, and I am glad. It makes me feel good to know that they care.

Lisa (*crying hard*). If we didn't care, Dora, when the group worker asked us if we would accept you up here again in this group, do you think we would have said yes? We had every opportunity to say *no*, but we wanted to give you a chance, Dora, to help you, and for God's sake, let us be helpful!

[Dora began to cry. This is the first time she is known to have broken down and cried; she had never been seen crying before. Group worker encouraged her to let herself go, saying that this was all right.]

Group worker (*to Dora*). That's the beginning.

Lisa. I didn't know you very long, Dora. I wasn't in that cottage very long, but I enjoyed coming out in the kitchen and helping you with the dishes, and underneath that big, bad front you put on, I knew you were just a little girl that wanted help —and didn't know how to ask for it. I used to be the same way, Dora. I believe that's why I thought so much of you, and because I felt, well, here's a chance . . . maybe I can help her straighten herself out. Dora, it is not too late. It is going to be harder than hell when you get out of that cell, but if you put your mind to it, you can . . . and not have to come back. Certainly people are not going to trust you for a long time, but if you stop and think, you've got to earn that trust. It's not easy in this damned place, I'll tell you that. It's not easy for the girls who try to be their best, because someone is always picking on them. But if you just reverse those big, tough feelings you've got and put as much will into being good as being bad, then you can. You've never seen me get this upset about any other girl in here, have you, Dora? No, it didn't bother me, because I didn't care. But

I thought a lot of you, Dora, and I'd never ever expected you to let people down again, especially after you got leniency that morning. There's something wrong, Dora, and as soon as you can realize it and accept it, you're helping yourself more than you'll ever know! See, Dora, when you can sit and cry just like you've been crying, you're not a big, bad girl at all; you're just human like the rest of us.

Rita. I have never been so happy in my life to see somebody cry! (*This was said softly and in a supportive way.*)

The next recording is a very short excerpt of the first group session with fifteen- and sixteen-year-old girls in a delinquency institution. It exemplifies their struggle with ethics and values and the group worker's intervention directed toward helping the girls to think for themselves.

The question of right and wrong came up during the early part of this meeting in connection with sexual relations and moved into the area of race relations where there was agreement that discrimination was wrong. It then moved into the area of killing.

Anna. It's hard to know what is right. I think there's nothing wrong with killing. When someone is hurting me, then it's not wrong.

[There was lively reaction to this statement; all the group members agreed except Cecile who spoke up for the first time and objected to what Anna had just said.]

Ruth. Yes, I get mad, and I also think I would kill when I think the person is wrong.

Group worker. I lived under the Nazis who said that one should kill Jews, mentally sick people, and crippled people, because they are worthless. What do you think about this?

Anna. But people can't help it if they are crippled. You should not kill them.

Group worker. Yes, *you* say that but they thought it was all right, and so they killed millions of people. Well, what do you think?

Anna (somewhat taken back and very thoughtful). Well, everybody can't just kill when he thinks it's right, but if someone killed my father I would have the right to kill them!

(*Freda nodded, but did not speak up.*)

Group worker. Well, let's think that one through. Have you ever heard of the Vendetta?

[The girls did not know this word, but were fascinated with something new. The group worker told them about the laws of the vendetta and compared it to a chain: Someone kills someone else, and so it continues.]

Anna. Well, what else can they do? There is nothing else but to continue killing.

Group worker. I don't know. In modern society we would ask someone to go before a court of law.

Jane. But the law may be wrong, too. How do we know it is right?

Group worker. Yes, the law can be wrong too. So, we need to think this through too. (*The meeting had to be terminated here because time had run out.*)

The following session shows the need for introspection, the wish to understand oneself. It was the third meeting of the same group of fifteen- to sixteen-year-old adolescent girls in a delinquency institution. Since one of the girls had run away, a new girl, Alma, had been taken into the group. This was her first meeting.

The group members had requested Alma's attendance. The group worker suggested that the girls bring her up-to-date on what had taken place at the previous meetings. Anna carried most of the explanation and soon swung the discussion back to what kind of person she wanted to be.

Anna. Being for real . . . being for real isn't something that happens when . . . I don't know. Being for real is a goal to me. You know.

Group worker. You mean to be a real person? (*Pause*) I just want to understand.

Anna. To be a real . . . yah. Somebody that . . .

Bea. To be honest and decent with everybody, rather than put on a false picture of yourself to anybody.

Anna. Be just—you know, when you say something, even in your thinking . . .

Alma. I think a lot of people are sincere in what they show other people about themselves. It's awfully hard to really stop and think about yourself and look at yourself objectively. The way other people do. I mean, you can think, you can try and really be honest with others, you know, as far as you know of yourself. But you never can be sure.

Bea. Sometimes you can't be sure of what you're doing. Yah . . .

Alma. Before you can be honest with everyone, you have to be completely honest with yourself and know yourself. And very few people know themselves, if any.

Anna. Yah.

Alma. People think they do, but they don't when it comes right down to it. Things come out in the open, and they didn't know they were there.

Bea. Who does, though?

Alma. Who can tell?

Bea. Who knows you, I mean?

Alma. Who knows me?

Bea. Yah.

Alma. Nobody knows me, and I know myself less than other people do probably.

Bea. That's one of those things. Well, you know . . . well . . . even your friends don't know you, you know. So . . .

Group worker. This is really hard. Last time you talked about two thngs: One, can we try to understand each other and ourselves? And two, what does it mean to be "on the top" and how does one get there? These were two different questions. Right? It doesn't matter which one we tackle first; whichever one you'd like.

Anna. Getting on top. That's what I'd like to talk about, and how to get there. If I don't get there, I don't want to be anywhere. If I don't reach the top, I don't want to be anywhere!

Group worker. Anna, what is it that you mean?

Anna. It's just if I can't be the best, I don't want to be anything, because then I don't feel . . . if you're not the best you're not worth anything.

Group worker. The best in what?

Anna. In everything.

Bea. In everything she does.

Anna. Everything.

Bea. Be on top as a housewife, if you want to be that.

Anna. Be on top of everything . . . anything and everything! Everything that you do. If you can't be on top, you may as well not do it. That's the way I feel. But then you have to work and strive to be at the top.

Alma. You have to take . . . now wait a minute! You see, you can never be completely on top. Maybe in your own eyesight, but not in everybody's eyesight. You may be the best prostitute in the United States of America, and you may be on top as far as that goes, but for somebody that has a job and who

doesn't believe in that, and believes in a nice, legal-type job, and
. . . they may not be on the top themselves, but you are on the
bottom as far as they're concerned.

Anna. Yes, that's right. That's right.

Alma. So you never really can be on top unless you're on top
in your own eyes, but . . .

Anna. I want to be on top in my own eyes, because . . .

Bea. Okay, that's a different thing.

Alma. What we were talking about—you know—I was thinking today . . . I was thinking today that this place up here, you
know . . . lots of times I think about it, and what it does for
you, and if it does anything for you. And I don't know. It just
seems like . . . to me, you know . . . it can't do anything. It
may not do anything at all. It can't do anything to harm me, so
the only thing it would do would be good. It can't do any more
harm to me as far as showing me some more ways to get into
trouble, because I know all of them. But you know, I know
girls who came up here at the same time I did, and they seemed
just sweet, such nice girls. They came from a small town, and
they didn't know a lot of stuff. They'd be up here for awhile;
they completely changed. And it wasn't for the better. I mean
. . . maybe in my eyes it was for the better, you know, but in
the general public's eyes it certainly wasn't.

Group worker. Was it in your eyes? Because you are an important person of the public, too!

Alma. In my eyes? I don't think it was for the better, because
I don't think they are happier for it, and to me, it doesn't make
any difference what you do as long as you're happy. If you're
happy, then it really doesn't make any difference.

Anna. That's the way I feel, too.

Alma. If you're happy, you should go out and do anything at
all. You know, if you're happy at robbing a bank, go and rob a
bank then.

Bea. At least you're happy at it.

Alma. Yah, but you see, the point is, are you really happy
though? Are you *really* happy? (*Laughter*)

Anna. Yah, but then you won't be happy going to jail.

Bea. Yah, I can see what you mean there; I can see what you
mean there.

Anna. You see, that's why you've got to know if you're happy
robbing a bank; if you are, then you're going to have to be happy
going to jail, too. If you keep robbing banks, you're going to go

to jail, so you've got to make sure you're going to be happy when you get in jail.

Alma. Yah, that's the thing. If you're going to lead the life of a bank robber . . .

Anna. Then you'll have to be happy both places.

Alma. And most people aren't, because I know—I know I'm not.

Group worker (turning to Anna). Would you be happy?

Anna. Oh, I'm happy every place I go.

Group worker. Really?

Anna. I make myself happy.

Bea. Yah, but you aren't happy here, though. You aren't happy.

Anna. I'm not happy to the fullest extent, because I can't do what I want to do. If I can't do what I want to do, I'll never be happy!

[Alma suggested that each group member tell whether she was happy and why, and what would make them happy. Ruth contributed first very little; Alice spoke up and said she would like to be an artist. The discussion shifted back to Ruth who said she was not happy because she didn't like to be locked up and because she wanted to do what she wanted to do. Alice commented that when Ruth did certain things, she was bound to be caught and get locked up. Ruth said she liked to get away with what she did. Ruth stayed on the surface in the discussion: she said she wanted to go out and party "cuz I don't like to stay in"; she did not want a job; she did not want to work; she intended to live off her mother until she got serious over a man and then she would go live off him.]

Group worker. Ruth, when I had a short talk alone with you, you were much more serious. Are you just trying to joke?

Ruth. I don't . . . I don't know. I think I want something, but then I . . . I always forget about it.

Group worker. Why?

Anna. Because you don't ever think you can reach it, do you?

Ruth. No, that's not it. I just change my mind too much.

Anna. You haven't made it up yet. Right? I understand that.

Bea. I understand that, too.

Anna. Because I remember I never had my mind made up one time either.

[Alma asked Anna if she was happy; Anna replied that she wasn't and explained that getting out of the institution, living with her girlfriend, getting a job, going through college, and achieving her goal as an architect would make her happy.]

Alma (turning to Bea). Are you happy, Bea?

Bea. Oh, no!

Alma. I know you're not, Bea.

Bea. I'm just the saddest girl that there is. I really am, really.

Alma. I know you are.

Bea. Oh, I've been happy—when I was in my younger days. Because I, you know, because I thought I was happy, because I thought I had everything, you know, that a girl my age should have. And I didn't really think like I do now. I think . . . I don't know. I think too much; I think of too many things, you know, which I shouldn't do. And I get awful confused. I would like . . . I would like to, if I really had a choice of what I do want . . . I don't want to be square in the way of saying that I just want to settle down and get married and just lead a normal life, you know, and have a nice family and have a nice marriage, and married friends. I don't just want to do that. But I don't want to be where I have to watch out for the law, either, because that's, that's . . .

Alma. Maybe you would like an exciting life?

Bea. I like an exciting life.

Alma. Maybe—maybe you can get into something like, something like night club work or something like that, where you could be within the law and yet get excitement too.

Anna. Maybe you'd like to travel, wouldn't you? Go to exciting places like Europe and Italy?

Bea. I like to travel.

Anna. All kinds of places, like Greece . . .

Alma. Maybe be a stewardess or something like that.

Bea. I'd like to be a designer, but it takes so many years of college.

Alma. Interior?

Bea. No, a dress designer.

Alma. Really?

Bea. Yah, I don't think I can go through all those years. I can't think of having to wait all those years, you know, having to go through without getting paid for any job, having to work my way up and start maybe at getting forty dollars a week, and maybe not even having a job at it. I can't see myself doing that, wasting that time.

Anna. This is hard.

Group worker. This is a very practical question. Have you ever checked what goes into learning this?

Bea. No, I haven't ever really checked into it. I know where I could probably go to school. But I know it's hard, because it's either you're there or else you're not anything. You either get a good job or you don't have a job at all in that field.

Alma. Yah, but they'll tell you after a certain length of time if they didn't think there was anything—that *you* had anything. I'm sure they'd tell you.

Bea. No, it's not that, it's not that, Alma. I mean the job itself . . . You either know the right people, and if you don't know them, you just don't get in. You don't get nowhere.

[Group worker promises Bea to check into job opportunities in the dress designing field.]

Alma. Do you think you could really stick to it, Bea?

Bea. Yah, I really do.

Alma. I mean, do you think you could give up all the people you know? You just have to give them up . . . you either have to break away completely or not break away at all.

Bea. Break away from what?

Alma. From the type of people you go around with, from the type of life.

Bea. Why? Why would I have to do that?

Alma. Because.

Bea. Probably from the type of life, Alma, but not from the people.

Alma. We . . . Bea, the people are part of the life, though.

Bea. Well, well, not the part ah . . . do you mean going against the law?

Alma. I mean the people, just the people that you associate with . . . the type of people. I know who they are.

Bea. Why would I have to let them go?

Alma. You couldn't mix the two. Maybe after you got the other ones, you wouldn't need them anymore. I don't know, but I know you can't mix the two. I know, because I've tried it.

Bea. Well, ah, I suppose if I had to stay out all night long and go to all the parties and everything, I couldn't be able to, but I wouldn't do that. And they don't interest me that much anymore anyway, the parties, I mean.

Alma. Yah, there are other things you enjoy doing. You can't go to school and get high. . . . A person who is going to do something reasonable with their life and who is going to work towards a goal, they don't drink and get high. They can't. Because they're realistic people, and they can't depend on some make-believe world when they're high.

Bea (with expression). Oh, now, "realistic!"

Anna. Oh heavens! You find people, Alma, millionaires, people that have reached their goal. They do, they feel that they do what they want to.

Alma. Sure, after you reach the goal then you can do what you want, but while you're getting there all you can do is work and . . . try to lead a normal type of life anyway. You can't run out in the streets and get high and all. . . .

Anna. Oh people! I wouldn't run out in the streets and get high!

Alma. I know . . . I know that if she was going to hold onto people like that, she'd be going to fashion school, or whatever it was, and then she'd get high and forget she was in fashion school. That's the way she is. And then it'd be gone, and when the people would say "Well, where is Bea?" and nobody would know where she was . . . and Bea would be over on the town someplace.

Group worker. But would Bea want it that way? Let Bea say it.

Alma. If Bea . . .

Group worker. Alma is making it tough for you, Bea. This is good.

Bea. Oh, I can see why Alma would think that, because it always happens to me, you know. . . . I'd go to school and everything and it overpowers me, having fun and—and getting high and going doing things that I know I'm not supposed to do. But then I enjoy doing things that I'm not supposed to do. I always have been that way too. But I really do go for this the mostest I've ever gone for anything. And I know I have for a whole lot of years; I haven't applied myself or really thought about going into anything, because I didn't have time, you know, and I couldn't think of going when I was . . .

Anna. Out!!!

Bea. When I was out . . . I couldn't think of going to school and trying to learn something. I couldn't do that. But I really would like to if I could, if I could settle down. That would be my goal—to do that.

Group worker. Alma's question is a very real one. She is saying, "Would it interest you that much? Can you give up certain other things?" Isn't this what you're saying?

(*Alma nodded in the affirmative.*)

Bea. It would interest me as for not going out like I had. But I wouldn't give up my friends entirely. I would probably cut a whole lot of them loose; I'd do that, but as for all of them . . . I wouldn't do that!

Alma. You know, though, these girls I've known in here . . . after all, you get so skeptical. I know, even through my own experiences, I've had so many good intentions, and I was going to go out and I wasn't going to let anything stand in my way! And I was going to do this and accomplish it, but maybe Bea is stronger than I am. Well, she is stronger than I am. I know that. But it's almost impossible to mix the two, because they're just like white and black or up and down. It's just completely opposites, and it is hard to do.

Anna. But you know, Alma, after you've had so many setbacks, you really learn. After so many set-backs you say, "Well, I've said this *so* many times!" But it's time to say, "Now here is something I *really* want to do!" *Then* there was no reason, but *now* there is a reason behind wanting to do this. You see? And you *can* go out there, and if you try . . . you can make it if you try. If you go out there and really want to do something, there is nothing in the world that can stop you. Getting high or not getting high. There is nothing that can stop you.

Bea. That's the whole point.

Anna. That's the whole point. If you want something badly enough, you will give up getting high.

Bea. That's right.

Alma. It comes to where you'd have to choose, you'd have to choose what is more important to you.

Bea. Well—how about all these . . . oh! I'm sure there are all these poets who get high, and there are a lot of people that get high who are "up there."

Alma. But don't you see, Bea, the reason that people get high . . . the reason people get high is that it's an escape. It's just like people get drunk. It's to get away, to escape the facts.

Bea. It's to get happy over something that . . . that you can't get happy . . . and you . . . ah . . .

Anna. That you can't jump up and rejoice for it. You get high, so you can really . . . you can be with yourself. You can have that deep joy.

Alma. It's a false happy though, it's a false happy. If you're doing something that you really want to do, that really means something to you . . . If it really meant something to Bea to design clothes, and that meant more than anything to her, that in itself would make her happy. She wouldn't need to get high. That's the last thing in the world she'd think about, because she'd be so happy doing something that meant something to her and giving her some gratification.

Bea. How about this? You have to start in, though, in order to really enjoy it. I have to go to school for awhile and really catch that field. Before that, well . . . well, I can't say it now, because I don't know, because I don't really know that much about it.

Alma. That's right.

Anna. She hasn't had a job.

Bea. So now I'd probably go out and get high, then afterwards I'd catch that deep feeling, and—and . . .

Anna. But you wouldn't need to get high.

Bea. I wouldn't need to get high anymore if I've got this job. I don't have it *now*.

Alma. Yah, but as long as you remember, Bea, that—that this one thing might hold something for you . . . When the going is hard and when it's not too interesting, don't just throw it over to go get high. You just have to remember . . .

Bea. Oh, I wouldn't. I wouldn't throw it over! I might perhaps say, "Well, it's going rough now, so I'm going out, and I'm going to get high tonight, because I feel bad over this, or I did this whole thing wrong, or else I got a bad grade or something!" So I go out and get high, but I wouldn't quit school. "I'm going to not bother about it no more," I wouldn't say that.

Anna. You see, Alma, the joy of getting this good feeling would come only when you start getting there, you start reaching your goal. You'd get that feeling then of getting there, of getting someplace. You wouldn't need to get high no more.

Alma. You know—this may sound corny, but they say—"A journey of a thousand miles begins by taking a single step." And everyday she goes to school, she is closer to her final goal.

Anna. And as long as she realizes that . . .

Alma (turning to Sue). What would make you happy, Sue? What would make you happy really?

Bea. I know you're not happy.

Sue. I know I'm not happy, too.

Anna. I know there's something you want, Sue. There is something you want, isn't there? Just say it.

Group worker. Sue, what is it?

Sue. Just to get a good job, as a secretary or something. I want to travel a lot.

Bea. How about your friends?

Anna. Are you going to school, Sue?

Alma. She's a senior and a junior both this year.

Sue. My friends? I'd give up some, but some I'd keep.

Bea. Who? You mean men friends? You mean your men friends?

Anna. What are you going to have when you get out of here? What do you want?

Bea. Your girlfriends now, you know, don't do anything at all for you. I mean, all they are is just going along with you and going out with you and not doing anything at all, not having a job or anything.

Anna. Who is that?

Bea. Your girlfriends.

Alma. You know what your men friends are doing for you? Nothing!

Bea. Men friends are either living off you, getting what they can off you, or going to a few parties with you.

Anna. Showing you off because you have nice pretty legs, pretty face, or a nice shape.

Alma. Or something like that.

Anna. You say that, because you know just about the same ones I do. You know what I mean. We've gone through that together.

Bea. So how about them?

Anna. What do you want when you get out of here? Do you want men or women? Or haven't you made up your mind?

Anna. You know, it's a hard . . . It was hard for me to make up my mind.

Bea. I don't think you have either, Anna.

Alma. You know what's hard? It's hard to give, you know. We all know . . . every girl in this room except maybe Ruth—I don't know the kind of people she knows—but . . . but the rest of us all know more or less the same kind of people in different degrees anyway. It's hard to think, well—I'll give them up because . . . because you can't just give them up, because you don't have anything to substitute with. Sometimes you think, "Well, well, they're not doing any good for me and never will do any good for me, and they really deep down don't care about me," but you don't have anything else.

Bea. I know there . . .

Anna (interrupting). But when you get something else, Alma, you really don't care about them.

Alma. I know when you get something else, but don't you understand that as long as you have them, you're not able to get anything else.

Anna. I have something else now.

Alma. What do you have now?

Anna. I have myself. I think I have somebody else.

Alma. I mean your friends. I mean your friends.

Anna. Oh friends! I don't think there really are very many true friends. And if you can't be true . . . acquaintances, I have lots of acquaintances. But friends, I have one.

Bea. Who is that?

Anna. I have one friend.

Bea. Who is your friend?

Anna. I have one. Her name is Maggie.

Bea. Is she a friend?

Anna. Yah.

Bea. A friend?

Anna. She's everything.

Bea. A woman lover?

Anna. That's right.

Alma. Do you know that in my whole life I've never been happy? In my whole life I can't think of ever having been happy.

Anna. You know, Alma, let me shake your hand, because I've never been happy either.

Alma. I've never been happy. Sometimes I think I enjoy being unhappy, even, because I don't—I can't be happy. So one has to get some kind of enjoyment, so I enjoy being unhappy.

Anna. The only time I was really happy was when I was taking heroin, but that was only for two minutes. Two minutes of happiness, and the rest was all sorrow. You know?

Alma. I've never been happy.

Bea. Oh, I've been happy in the sense of enjoying myself you know, but as for really being deep down happy about what I'm doing about—about if it's right and everything . . . Is anybody happy for me that I'm doing this? Well . . . well . . . that has never been, because I have never been. Where I'm happy, no one else is happy, you know—as far as my people are concerned.

Anna. You see, I'm happy in thinking that I can be happy in a couple more months, or maybe a month, you know.

Bea. As for being out, you mean?

Anna. Yes. Out, going to school, and getting someplace. Then I keep thinking, "Well, I'm happy now, because I just know I'm going to get there" you know. I just know eventually I'm going to get there, and you know, you just get happy in thinking that one of these days you're going to be complete.

Bea. Oh, I've been happy at thinking that, well, "I'll be going out, and I'll be getting home, and I won't be having to bother to come back here and everything," but it's not really, really happy.

Anna. It's not being happy then.

Bea. It's happy from being—it's happy from being away from up here. . . . I mean anything is happy from here, you know. I'm going off grounds. I'm happy for it. If I'm going to recreation, I'm happy for it. But that's not really happy.

Alma. Can you be really satisfied? Be happy with your life, with the way you are, with everything else?

Bea. Everything, everything at all?

Anna. There was once when I was happy like that, Alma.

Bea. When was that?

Anna. For three months.

Bea. When was that?

Anna. When I was pregnant. I was very happy and very content with everything that happened to me.

Alma. I don't know what I want.

Anna. When I was pregnant, I couldn't explain it. It was . . . you know . . . you just kept thinking . . . well, you know, "I'm doing something." You know. "This time I'm not just messing around or going out to a party or getting dressed to look good. I'm developing something that God has made. God made man, and I'm making one too." I mean, it's just an extraordinary feeling.

Alma. Do you think though that you got . . . When we talked about being happy and what you're going to do, you say, "Well, I'm going to go out and get a job and be a secretary" or "I'm going to go out and go to school and that" but how good are you going to do it? I don't think any of them will, if you want to know my honest opinion.

Group worker. But Alma, Anna has said something that I think we should hear. She said that she was once happy, when she was creating something.

Anna. Yah.

Group worker. Anna, I think this is also what you are thinking about when you say you want to become an architect. This is creating. You talk about more than just having a job.

Anna. I've had jobs. They are nothing. You just get paid, you know, and you go out and buy some new clothes and you party. You go back to work and then you get some more money. I mean, it's just so routine. You get so sick of doing the same thing over and over. You go out and get . . . I never got sick of getting high, you know, but it's just that you can't stay high all the time.

Alma. I do! I do! It just doesn't mean anything any more to me! Sure, it's exciting to do it once. Just like I couldn't wait until I looked old enough where I could go to all the joints in town without having them put me out. I just couldn't wait. Then after I got there it wasn't anything but just a lot of stupid people, and it didn't mean anything at all. . . . That's the way it is. Just like you think, "Well I'll get drunk," or something like that. It seems like a good idea when you're younger, or for awhile. But later you know that when you're not drunk anymore, everything is going to be the same as it was before. So why even bother? That's the way I am.

Bea. That's the way I am, too. I can get bored awful fast too, with people and with almost everything.

Anna. I get bored with people when they're always trying to do the same thing, or copying one another. I get very bored when . . .

Alma. Yah, they're not very imaginative people.

Anna. Yah, I just . . . People that have a creative imagination, you know or with just a hell of an imagination just fascinate me, you know, just to my fullest.

Group worker. Alma, is there something you would like to create? Bea said that drawing is creation, and you said something about painting. It's an interesting thing that so many of you like this. Is there something in you that you would like to express?

Alma. There are little things—moments—that I enjoy myself. I like to write, and I like to act, and I enjoy looking at other types of painting, you know—art and things like that—to see other people's ideas. But I don't know . . . it doesn't . . . it's not that much of a . . . I don't know if it's really a part of me. I never really . . . It's satisfying to me, you know, but it's not . . . I don't know. It doesn't mean that much—nothing means anything to me really. I don't care about anything. I don't have any religion. Religion means nothing to me at all. Lot of times I think I would like to be religious, because then when everything else is down, you can say, "Well, at least I have God." You know you still have something to believe in. I don't. There's nothing in this world that means anything to me. I believe in loyalty. That's about the only thing. But I've been so . . . so let down by people that I've believed in, that that doesn't even mean very much anymore.

Anna. That is right.

Group worker. Is there anything that kind of cries in you that wants to come out?

Alma. All I want is to be happy, and I doubt if I ever will. Just now I'm to the point where I just don't care about anything. The only thing I want is to want something . . . and I don't even want anything. I can't think of anything I even want that would make me happy. Sometimes I think I want . . .

Bea. You want a good man.

Alma. That . . . that means something to me: to have a man, to have a man who loves me, and I love him; if I had that I think I would be happy. That means even if I had to live in a shack or out in the grass; it wouldn't make any difference.

Bea. I'm not that way at all.

Alma. That means everything to me, I think.

Group worker. That's something creative too, Alma.

Anna. I think so too.

Group worker. To like a human being: I think that is something creative.

Alma. Oh, that's just a wonderful feeling.

Bea. I wish I could feel that way, but I don't.

Alma. I feel that way, but it's even worse if you feel that way and you don't have it. If it didn't bother you at all, you wouldn't even think about it. But if you feel that way and you don't have it, it's even worse. If it means more to you than anything, and you can't have it, and you just never will have it, well, then it doesn't mean anything at all.

Bea. Well, you can't say, "I will never have it."

Alma. I know I won't, though, because I know myself. Because I know how I am. Because I let people misuse me and because I can't have it, I substitute something else, and by substituting something else, I'll never be in a position to get it.

Bea. Yah.

Alma. When you've led the kind of life I've had, you do it because you don't have anything else, and that's all you've got, so you have to do it. And by the very fact that you're doing it, you'll never get anything else, because you'll never be there where the rest of it is.

Bea. That's right, that's right. (*Turns to Anna*) She's the same way, and you too. (*Turns to Sue*) A secretary. I doubt if you'll ever be a secretary. If you do, it'll be ten years from now when your whole outlook has changed.

BIBLIOGRAPHY

Family and Socialization

Bettelheim, Bruno. "Growing Up Female," *Harper's Magazine,* CCXXV, No. 1349 (October 1962), 120-23.

Bronfenbrenner, Urie. "The Changing American Child," in Eli Ginzberg, ed., *Values and Ideals of American Youth,* New York: Columbia University Press, 1961, pp. 71-84.

Brownlee, Aleta. "The American Indian Child," *Children,* V, No. 2 (March-April 1958), 55-60.

Faegre, M. E. *The Adolescent in Your Family,* U.S. Department of Health Education, and Welfare, Social Security Administration, Children's Bureau, 1954.

Frank, Mary and Lawrence K. *Your Adolescent at Home and in School,* New York: The Viking Press, Inc., 1956.

Frazier, E. Franklin. "The Impact of Urban Civilization Upon Negro Family Life" in Bell and Vogel, eds., *A Modern Introduction to the Family,* New York: Free Press of Glencoe, 1960, pp. 103-11.

Kagan, Henry E. "Teaching Values to Our Children," in Eli Ginzberg, ed., *Values and Ideals of American Youth,* New York: Columbia University Press, 1961, pp. 255-70.

Kaufman, Irving; Alice L. Peck and Consuelo K. Tagiuri. "The Family Constellation and Overt Incestuous Relations Between Father and Daughter," in Bell and Vogel, eds., *A Modern Introduction to the Family,* New York: Free Press of Glencoe, 1960, pp. 544-54.

Kobrin, Solomon. "The Impact of Cultural Factors on Selected Problems of Adolescent Development in the Middle and Lower Class," *American Journal of Orthopsychiatry,* XXXII, No. 3 (April 1962), 387-90.

Robey, Ames; Richard J. Rosenwald, John E. Snell and Rita E. Lee. "The Runaway Girl: A Reaction to Family Stress," *American Journal of Orthopsychiatry,* XXXIV, No. 4 (July 1964), 762-67.

Spock, Benjamin, M.D., *Problems of Parents,* Boston: Houghton Mifflin Company, 1962.

Child and Adolescent Development: General

Blos, Peter. *On Adolescence*. New York: Free Press of Glencoe, Inc., 1962 (see especially pp. 230-44).

Campbell, Robert J., III., M.D. "Sex and the Teenager," in William C. Bier, S.J. *The Adolescent, His Search for Understanding*, New York: Fordham University Press, 1963, pp. 28-38.

Cole, Luella and Irma Nelson Hall. *Psychology of Adolescence* (6th ed.), New York: Holt, Rinehart and Winston, Inc., 1964.

Deutsch, Helen, M.D. *The Psychology of Women*, New York: Grune & Stratton, Inc., 1944.

Frank, Lawrence K.; Ross Harrison, Elisabeth Hellersberg, Karen Machover, and Meta Steiner. Personality Development in Adolescent Girls, Monographs of the Society for Research in Child Development, Inc. XVI, Serial No. 53, 1951, New Orleans, La., Child Development Publications, 1953.

Havighurst, Robert J. and Hilda Taba. *Adolescent Character and Personality*, New York: John Wiley & Sons, Inc., 1949.

Josselyn, Irene M., M.D. *The Adolescent and His World*. New York: Family Service Association of America, 1952.

———. "The Cider Adolescent," in Eli Ginzberg, ed., *Values and Ideals of American Youth*, New York: Columbia University Press, 1961. pp. 27-35.

Kluckholn, Clyde and Henry A. Murray. *Personality in Nature, Society and Culture*, New York: Alfred A. Knopf, Inc., 1949 (a good basic reference).

Konopka, Gisela and Jack V. Wallinga. "Stress as a Social Problem," *American Journal of Orthopsychiatry*, XXXIV, No. 3 (April 1964), 536-42.

Maier, Henry W. *Three Theories of Child Development*, New York: Harper & Row, Publishers, 1965.

Schutz, Richard E. "Patterns of Personal Problems of Adolescent Girls," in Lester D. and Alice Crow, eds., *Readings in Child and Adolescent Psychology*, New York: David McKay Co., Inc. 1961, pp. 339-45.

Taylor, Harold. "The Ambiguities of Public Morality: A Problem for World Youth," in R. M. MacIver, ed., *Dilemmas of Youth: In America Today*, New York: Harper and Brothers, 1961, pp. 113-25.

Child and Adolescent Development: Conflict Between Generations

Bettelheim, Bruno. "The Problem of Generations," in Erik H. Erikson, ed., *Youth: Change and Challenge,* New York: Basic Books, Inc., 1963, pp. 64-92.

Pearson, Gerald H. J., M.D. *Adolescence and the Conflict of Generations,* New York: W. W. Norton & Co., Inc., 1958.

Child and Adolescent Development: Identification, Independence and Isolation

Bauer, Francis C. "Problems of Dependence and Independence," in William C. Bier, S.J., *The Adolescent: His Search for Understanding,* New York: Fordham University Press, 1963, pp. 145-51.

Erikson, Erik H. *Identity and the Life Cycle,* selected papers, *Psychological Issues,* I, No. 1 (1959), Monograph 1 (complete issue).

Schneiders, Alexander A. "The Adolescent's Search for Identity," in William C. Bier, S.J. *The Adolescent: His Search for Understanding,* New York: Fordham University Press, 1963, pp. 145-51.

Zilbach, Joan, M.D. "Profile of a Socially Deprived Girl," in *Girls in Crisis,* Proceedings of the Conference sponsored jointly by The Group Work Council, Welfare, Federation of Cleveland, and The School of Applied Social Sciences, Western Reserve University, Cleveland, Ohio, May 19, 1962, pp. 34-42.

Child and Adolescent Development: Self-Image

Anderson, Camilla M. "The Self-Image: A Theory of the Dynamics of Behavior," in Lester D. and Alice Crow, eds., *Readings in Child and Adolescent Psychology,* New York: David McKay Co., Inc., 1961, pp. 406-19.

Frank, Anne. *The Diary of a Young Girl,* New York: Modern Library, Inc., 1952.

McCann, Richard V. "The Self-Image and Delinquency: Some Implications for Religion," *Federal Probation*, XX, No. 3 (September 1956), 14-23.

Cultural Deprivation

Keller, Suzanne. "The Social World of the Urban Slum Child: Some Early Findings," *American Journal of Orthopsychiatry*, XXXIII, No. 5 (October 1963), 823-31.

Miller, Walter B. "Lower Class Culture as a Generating Milieu of Gang Delinquency," in Marvin V. Wolfgang, Leonard Savitz, and Norman Johnston, eds., *The Sociology of Crime and Delinquency*, New York: John Wiley and Sons, Inc., 1962, pp. 267-76.

Riessman, Frank. *The Culturally Deprived Child*, New York: Harper & Row, Publishers, 1962.

The Social Scene and Cultural Change: General

Abramovitz, Moses. "Growing Up in an Affluent Society," in Eli Ginzberg, ed., *The Nation's Children*, I, 158-79. New York: Columbia University Press, 1960.

Annals of the American Academy of Political and Social Science. *Teenage Culture*, CCCXXXVIII, November 1961.

Babin, Pierre. *Crisis of Faith*, New York: Herder and Herder, 1963.

Cohen, Eli E. "New Opportunities Awaiting Contemporary Youth," in R. M. MacIver, ed., *Dilemmas of Youth: In America Today*, New York: Harper & Row, Publishers, 1961, pp. 127-31.

Davis, Kingsley, "Adolescence and Social Structure," in Jerome M. Seidman, ed., *The Adolescent—A Book of Readings*, Revised Edition, New York: Holt, Rinehart, & Winston, Inc., 1960, pp. 42-50.

Erhmann, Winston W. "Changing Sexual Mores," in Eli Ginzberg, ed., *Values and Ideals of American Youth*, New York: Columbia University Press, 1961, pp. 53-70.

Goodman, Paul. *Growing Up Absurd*, New York: Random House, 1960.

Hollingshead, August B. "Some Crucial Tasks Facing Youth: Problems of Adolescence, Peer Group, and Early Marriage," in R. M. MacIver, ed., *Dilemmas of Youth: in America Today*, New York: Harper & Row, Publishers, 1961, pp. 15-30.

Keniston, Kenneth. "Social Change and Youth in America," in Erik H. Erikson, ed., *Youth: Change and Challenge*, New York: Basic Books, Inc., 1963, pp. 161-87.

Kirkendall, Lester A. *Premarital Intercourse and Interpersonal Relationships,* New York: The Julian Press, Inc., 1961.

Loomis, Earl A., Jr., M.D. "The Significance of Religious Development," in Eli Ginzberg, ed., *Values and Ideals of American Youth,* New York: Columbia University Press, 1961, pp. 103-21.

Mead, Margaret, "The Young Adult," in Ginzberg, ed., *Values and Ideals of American Youth,* op. cit., pp. 37-51.

Smith, Ernest A., *American Youth Culture,* New York: Free Press of Glencoe, 1962.

"Youth in a Violent Age," in Grant S. McClellan, ed., *Juvenile Delinquency,* The Reference Shelf, XXVIII. No. 2. New York: The H. W. Wilson Co., 1956.

The Social Scene and Cultural Change: Women

Cassara, Beverly Menner, ed., *American Women: The Changing Image,* Boston: Beacon Press, 1962.

de Beauvoir, Simone. *The Second Sex,* H. M. Parshley, trans. and ed., New York: Bantam Books, 1952.

Cohen, Dorothy. *The Fascinating Female,* Glen Rock, N.J.: Paulist Press, 1960.

Frieden, Betty. *The Feminine Mystique,* New York: Dell Publishing Co., Inc., 1963.

Kinsey, Alfred O., Wardelle B. Pomeroy and Clyde E. Martin; *Sexual Behavior in the Human Female,* Philadelphia: W. B. Saunders Co., 1953.

Mead, Margaret. *Male and Female,* New York: William Morrow & Co., Inc., 1949.

Moser, Clarence G. *Understanding Girls,* New York: Association Press, 1957 (see especially Chapter 2, "The Feminine Role in Our Culture Today").

President's Commission on the Status of Women. *American Women,* Report of the President's Commission on the Status of Women, 1963, Washington, D.C.: U.S. Government Printing Office, 1963.

Ware, Caroline F. *Women Today: Trends and Issues in the United States* (pamphlet), New York: National Board of the YWCA of the USA, 1963.

The World of Work

Bell, Howard M. "Out-of-School Youth Tell Their Story," in Jerome M. Seidman, ed., *The Adolescent—A Book of Readings,* Revised Edition, New York: Holt, Rinehart & Winston, Inc., 1960, pp. 61-66.

Dansereau, H. Kirk. "Work and the Teenager," *The Annals of the American Academy of Political and Social Science,* CCCXXXVIII, November 1961, 44-52.

Ellingston, John R. *Youth Without Jobs—A National Emergency,* a discussion paper prepared for the Governor's Conference on Children and Youth, Minneapolis, Minnesota, April 23-24, 1962, 52 pp. mimeo.

Freeman, Mary. "The Marginal Sex," The Commonweal, LXXV, No. 19 (February 1962), 483-86.

Gilbreth, Lillian M. "Women in Industry," in Beverly Benner, ed., *American Women: The Changing Image,* Boston: Beacon Press, 1962, pp. 90-98.

Meade, Martin J. "Educational Choices in Adolescence," in William C. Bier, S.J., *The Adolescent: His Search for Understanding,* New York: Fordham University Press, 1963, pp. 196-205.

United States Department of Labor. *Training Opportunities for Women and Girls,* Women's Bureau Publication No. 274, 1960 (see entire series, entitled *The Outlook for Women*).

Unmarried Mothers

Bernstein, Rose. "The Deprived Teenage Unmarried Mother," in *Girls in Crisis,* Proceedings of the Conference sponsored jointly by The Group Work Council, Welfare Federation of Cleveland, and The School of Applied Social Sciences, Western Reserve University, Cleveland, Ohio, May 19, 1962, pp. 52-64.

———. "The Maternal Role in the Treatment of Unmarried Mothers," *Social Work,* I, No. 8 (January 1963), 58-65.

Child Welare League of America. *Standards for Services to Unmarried Parents,* New York: Child Welfare League of America, Inc., (Booklet UM-13).

Garland, Patricia. "The Community's Part in Preventing Illegitimacy," *Children,* X, No. 2 (March-April 1963), 71-75.

Herzog, Elizabeth. "Unmarried Mothers: Some Questions to be Answered and Some Answers to be Questioned," Child Welfare, XLI, No. 8, (October 1962), 339-50.

Katz, Sanford N. "Legal Protections for the Unmarried Mother and Her Child," *Children*, X, No. 2 (March-April 1963), 55-59.

Kronick, Jane C. "An Assessment of Research Knowledge Concerning the Unmarried Mother," in *Research Perspectives on the Unmarried Mother*, New York: Child Welfare League of America, Inc., September 1962, pp. 17-31.

Delinquency: General

Bloch, Herbert A. and Arthur Neiderhoffer. *The Gang: A Study in Adolescent Behavior*, New York: Philosophical Library, 1958.

Cloward, Richard A. and Lloyd E. Ohlin, *Delinquency and Opportunity*, New York: Free Press of Glencoe, 1960.

Cohen, Albert K. *Delinquent Boys—The Culture of the Gang*, New York: Free Press of Glencoe, 1955 (see especially pp. 45-46 and 138-47, re: female delinquency).

Ellingston, John R. *Protecting Our Children From Criminal Careers*, Englewood Cliffs, N.J., Prentice-Hall, Inc., 1948.

Grant, Marguerite Q. and Martin Warren. "Alternates to Institutionalization,"*Children*, X, No. 4 (July-August 1963), 147-52.

Hathaway, Starke R. and Elio D. Monachesi. *Adolescent Personality and Behavior—M.M.P.I. Patterns of Normal, Delinquent, Dropout, and Other Outcomes*, Minneapolis: University of Minnesota Press, 1963.

Konopka, Gisela. "Adolescent Delinquent Girls," in *Children*, XI, No. 1 (January-February 1964), 21-26.

Kvaraceus, William D., Walter B. Miller, et al. *Delinquent Behavior— Culture and the Individual*, Washington, D.C.: Juvenile Delinquency Project, National Education Association of the United States, 1959.

Robison, Sophia M. *Juvenile Delinquency: Its Nature and Control*, New York: Holt, Rinehart & Winston, Inc., 1960.

Salisbury, Harrison E. *The Shook-Up Generation*, New York: Harper & Row, Publishers, 1958.

U.S. Department of Health, Education and Welfare. *Juvenile Delinquency Services*, Welfare Administration, Children's Bureau Publication No. 421, 1964.

Witmer, Helen L. and Ruth Kotinsky, eds., *New Perspectives for Research on Juvenile Delinquents*, U.S. Department of Health, Education and Welfare, Children's Bureau Publication No. 356, Washington, D.C. 1956.

Delinquency: Problems and Practices of

Institutional Treatment

Aichhorn, August. *Wayward Youth,* New York: The Viking Press, Inc., 1935.

Augustine, Brother, F.S.C. "The Institutional Approach to Delinquency," in Willim C. Bier, S.J., *The Adolescent: His Search for Understanding,* New York: Fordham University Press, 1963, pp. 114-21.

Clendenen, Richard. "To Synchronize the Training School Program with Life in the Community," *The Child,* XIV, No. 5 (November 1949), 73-77.

Deutsch, Albert. *Our Rejected Children,* Boston: Little, Brown & Co., 1950.

Halleck, Seymour L., M.D. and Marvin Hersko. "Homosexual Behavior in a Correctional Institution for Adolescent Girls," *American Journal of Orthopsychiatry,* XXXII, No. 5 (October 1962), 911-17.

Konopka, Gisela. *Group Work in the Institution,* New York: Association Press, 1954 (see especially Chapter VI, "Social Group Work in Institutions for Juvenile Delinquents," pp. 185-251).

————. "What Houseparents Should Know," Children, III, No. 2 (March-April 1956), 49-54.

Mayer, Morris F. "The Houseparents and the Group Living Process," in Schulze, Susanne, ed., *Creative Group Living in the Children's Institution.* New York: Association Press, 1951, pp. 97-116.

National Conference on Prevention and Control of Juvenile Delinquents. *Report on Institutional Treatment of Delinquent Juveniles,* Washington, D.C.: U.S. Government Printing Office, 1947.

National Council on Crime and Delinquency. *Standards and Guides for the Detention of Children and Youth,* (2nd ed.), New York, 1961.

Papanek, Ernst. "The Training School: It's Program and Leadership," Federal Probation, XX, No. 2 (June 1953) 16-22.

Redl, Fritz and David Wineman. *The Aggressive Child,* New York: Free Press of Glencoe, 1957.

Toigo, Romolo. "Illegitimate and Legitimate Cultures in a Training School for Girls," (the "make-believe family"), undated, mimeo, 31 pp.

U.S. Department of Health, Education and Welfare. *Institutions Serving Delinquent Children—Guides and Goals,* Children's Bureau Publication No. 360, Revised Edition, 1962.

Use of Groups in Treatment

Alpern, Evelyn, Chairman. "Treatment of the Adolescent—Workshop, 1960," *American Journal of Orthopsychiatry,* XXXII, No. 3 (April 1962), 383-403.

Berman, Netta. "The Group Worker in a Children's Institution," in Susanne Schulze, ed. *Creative Group Living in the Children's Institution,* New York: Association Press, 1951, pp. 117-23.

Cohen, A. Alfred. "Use of Group Process in an Institution," *Social Work,* I, No. 4 (October 1956), 57-61.

Fogel, David. "Use of Groups in a Juvenile Hall," *Corrective Psychiatry and Journal of Social Therapy,* X, No. 5, September 1964.

Gabriel, Betty. "Group Treatment for Adolescent Girls," *American Journal of Orthopsychiatry,* XIV, No. 4, October 1944, 593-602.

Hersko, Marvin. "Group Psychotherapy with Delinquent Adolescent Girls," *American Journal of Orthophychiatry,* XXXII, No. 1, January 1962, pp. 169-75.

Klein, Alan F. "Individual Change Through Group Experience," *Social Welfare Forum,* 1959, New York: Columbia University Press, 1959, pp. 136-55.

Konopka, Gisela. *Social Group Work: A Helping Process,* Englewood Cliffs, N.J.: Prentice-Hall, Inc., 1963.

———. "Social Group Work Method: Its Use in the Correctional Field," *Federal Probation,* XLV, No. 1, March 1950.

———. *Therapeutic Group Work with Children,* Minneapolis: University of Minnesota Press, 1949 (see especially pp. 93-133).

Maier, Henry, ed., *Group Work as Part of Residential Treatment,* New York: National Association of Social Workers, 1965.

Pearl, Arthur. "The Halfway House: The Focal Point of a Model Program for the Rehabilitation of Low Income Offenders," in Riessman, Cohen, and Pearl, eds., *Mental Health of the Poor,* New York: Free Press of Glencoe, 1964, pp. 497-508.

Richards, Catharine V. "The Place of Group Experience in the Life of a Socially Deprived Girl," in *Girls in Crisis,* Proceedings of the Conference sponsored jointly by The Group Work Council, Welfare Federation of Cleveland, and The School of Applied Social Sciences, Western Reserve University, Cleveland, Ohio, May 19, 1962, pp. 34-42.

Scheidlinger, Saul. "Experiential Group Treatment of Severely Deprived Latency-Age Children," in Riessman, Cohen, and Pearl, eds. *Mental Health of the Poor,* New York: Free Press of Glencoe, 1964, pp. 348-61.

Sequin, Mary; Josephine Daugherty and Sarah Short. "Working with Girls Who are Unable to Respond to Conventional Group Services," in *Girls in Crisis,* op. cit., pp. 83-94.

Wiltse, Kermit T. "Orthophychiatric Programs for Socially Deprived Groups," *American Journal of Orthopsychiatry*, XXXIII, No. 5 (October 1963), 806-13.

INDEX

TWENTIETH CENTURY VIEWS

American Authors

TWENTIETH CENTURY VIEWS

British Authors

TWENTIETH CENTURY VIEWS

European Authors